1.2.3.4.5.6.7.8.9.

ALL ABOUT NUMEROLOGY

Lia Robin

ALL ABOUT

Numerology

Astrolog Publishing House

1.2.3.4.5.6.7.8.9.   .9.8.7.6.5.4.3.2.1

Editor: Lia Robin

Cover Design: Na'ama Yaffe

Layout and Graphics: Marla Bentham

Production Manager: Dan Gold

P. O. Box 1123, Hod Hasharon 45111, Israel

Tel: 972-9-7412044

Fax: 972-9-7442714

E-Mail: info@astrolog.co.il

Astrolog Web Site: www.astrolog.co.il

©Astrolog Publishing House Ltd. 2001

ISBN 965-494-109-0

Published by Astrolog Publishing House 2001

Printed in Israel

10 9 8 7 6 5 4 3 2 1

Table of Contents

Part 1:

Introduction

7

Part 2:

Day-to-Day Prediction

91

Part 3:

The Winning Number!
Numerological Compatibility

175

Some of the contents of this book were taken from:
Day-By-Day Numerology by Lia Robin
(Astrolog Publishing House Ltd., 1998)
Little Big Book of Basic Numerology by Lia Robin
(Astrolog Publishing House Ltd., 1998)

Introduction

א	ב	ג	ד	ה	ו	ז	ח	ט	י	יא	יב	כ	כא	ק	וכק
A	B	Γ	Δ	E	F	Z	H	Θ	I	IA	I9	K	KA	P	PKF
I	II	III	IV	V	VI	VII	VIII	IX	X	XI	XIX	XX	XXI	C	CXXVI
1	2	3	4	5	6	7	8	9	10	11	19	20	21	100	126

Numerology, the theory of numbers, is a simple method of character analysis and predicting the future. On a higher level, the theory of numbers offers a system for understanding the true nature of the universe.

Numerology, like other methods of prediction, maintains that an ordering principle exists, above and beyond the range of natural phenomena, and offers an explanation of the many details and events we experience, based on a clear-cut set of principles.

Modern numerology is based on Pythagorean and Kabbalistic principles, but is also inflenced by the Christian numerical symbolism of the Middle Ages and by attempts in the Renaissance to bridge the pagan and Christian worlds - between classical philosophy and Christian culture.

Western numerology is based on the Pythagorean principle. This states that reality is constructed mathematically, and that all phenomena are in fact numbers. Hence, each individual's character and destiny may be expressed in numbers. This constitutes the first of the main principles of popular numerology; the second asserts that a person's name (and indeed the name of each thing) contains his true essence.

Your name, according to this magic theory, is not just a random label. Your name *is* your identity. Your name is likely to disclose who you really are.

Numerology converts your name into numerals, and analyzes your personality by interpreting the numbers according to set rules.

Each letter of the alphabet is connected to a specific number:

```
1  2  3  4  5  6  7  8  9
A  B  C  D  E  F  G  H  I
J  K  L  M  N  O  P  Q  R
S  T  U  V  W  X  Y  Z
```

In order to locate your number (in other words, the number of your name), write down your first and last names and convert each letter into its corresponding number. Next, add up all the numbers. If the sum has two digits, add them together, and keep adding until you are left with a single-digit number. This is your number.

For example: JOHN DOE

J	1	D	4
O	6	O	6
H	8	E	5
N	5		

The sum of JOHN is
$1 + 6 + 8 + 5 = 20 = 2 + 0 = 2$,
the sum of DOE is
$4 + 6 + 5 = 15 = 1 + 5 = 6$,
and the combination of JOHN DOE (2+6) gives a total of 8.

Numerologists claim that the full name given to you at birth reflects the mysterious forces acting in the universe, as well as your destiny. Nicknames and other names reflect your image in the eyes of those who gave you those names.

A woman's maiden name indicates her character before marriage. Later, her married name is likely to disclose how married life has affected her.

Another important number for numerologists is the birth number, the number resulting from the combination of the numerals contained in one's birth date. If you were born, for example, on 8/7/1995, your birth number would be:

$8 + 7 + 1 + 9 + 9 + 5 = 39 = 3 + 9 = 12 = 1 + 2 = 3$

This number reflects your character and destiny, as they were forged by the universal powers operating at the time of your birth. This number may or may not match your name number. If the two numbers do not match, you can expect to experience many inner conflicts.

If the day and month of your birth are combined with each year, it will give you your personal number for the year.

For example, if your birthday is April 1st, and the year is 1980, your number for that year will be 5 ($1 + 4 + 1 + 9 + 8 = 23 = 5$). It will be a year of changes and new experiences, and perhaps a year of ardent love as well. However, by adding up the numbers for the same date in 1981, you would get number 6, representing a quiet, domestic and peaceful year.

For a more in-depth analysis, numerologists recommend breaking the name down into separate letters, checking how many times each letter (or number) appears, and which letters (or numbers) are missing. The repetition of a certain number indicates that the major characteristic of that number is very strongly expressed in that individual. The lack of a particular number indicates that the trait characterized by that number is missing.

Each and every number is associated with a comprehensive symbolism of its own, which subsequently also determines the characteristic traits of individuals connected to that number.

The number 1, the first of all numbers, and the number of which all other numbers are composed, is considered in many religious and mystic traditions to symbolize God, the primal cause, the source of all things, and the unity of the entire universe. Therefore, numerology assigns to number 1 people characteristics associated with the Christian Father-God. People who are creative, those with initiative or a tendency toward organization or technology are characterized by number 1. This number relates to the image of God as Creator. The power, control, leadership, isolation, intolerance toward opponents and generosity expressed toward supporters are all characteristics taken from the image of God as portrayed in the Old and New Testaments.

The number 2 symbolizes femininity. It is the first of the even numbers, considered in the numerological tradition as female, as opposed to the odd numbers, which are identified with masculinity.

Historically, men have been dominant in most societies. This may be the reason why the odd numbers were associated with the masculine and the good, and the even numbers with the feminine. Therefore, people with 2 as their number are said to have characteristics connected to traditional notions of femininity: they are passive and obey authority figures.

The number 2 is also the number that represents the devil. He is "evil" since he is the first number to break the unity and totality of number 1, and bring plurality and dissent into the world. With the advent of number 2, duality, contrast and antagonism are born.

The synthesis of these contrasts and the mending of the fracture represented by number 2, come into play with number 3.

The number 3 has many symbols and is connected to the triangle, the first shape to enclose space. Just as number 1 symbolized wholeness and totality, and number 2, division and contrast, so number 3 represents harmony, creativity, self-expression and visible manifestations of God. (In the Holy Trinity – the Father, Son and Holy Spirit – the number 3 is associated with the Holy Spirit floating over the primordial waters and creating the world.)

All of the above is strengthened by the sexual symbolism of the number 3. It is the first number with a central phallic focus, as well as the contrasts of man (1) and woman (2) united in sex (3).

And indeed, the characteristics of power, action, creativity, love of pleasure, attractiveness, attraction to members of the other sex and a constant need for admiration and affection are attributed to number 3.

The number 3 is considered the luckiest of numbers and represents good and the most perfect. (The third degree of comparison – going from "good" to "better" to "best" – is also the highest.)

The number 3 stands for the totality of a thing, just as it represents the optimum. Each phenomenon has a beginning, a middle and an end; time is divided into three components: past, present and future; space is divided into, length, breadth and thickness.

The number 3 frequently appears in folktales and nursery rhymes: three wishes, three chances, three brothers, three bears, and three little pigs.

The number 3 is also the most important number in magic, where it represents perfection.

Three repetitions of an oath or spell represent total repetition or "all possible repetitions" of the oath or spell. In Greek mythology, there are many groups of three: the Three Graces, the Three Goddesses of Revenge, and the Three Goddesses of Fate.

The number 4 is associated with the simplest stable form, and is therefore the number of tangible and material things particularly affiliated with the earth.

According to an ancient belief popular in Europe until the 17th century, and still preserved in different versions by those who practice the occult, all existing things are composed of four elements: fire, air, earth and water. There are four seasons in a year.

The traits of heaviness and boredom linked to number 4 people stem from the same concept of stability associated with that number. In addition, the affinity between number 4 and the earth and material substances resulted in this number's affiliation with gloom and failure, since in the classical and medieval eras, it was commonly believed that life on earth, the material world, was an oppressive prison from which the soul was liberated at death.

The number 5 stands at the halfway point between 1 and 9. It is therefore associated with the characteristics of restlessness, irresponsibility, and multifariousness. The fact that human beings have five senses determines the character of number 5: vitality, sensuality, sexuality and nervousness.

Number 5 is composed of 1 (God) and 4 (matter) and is a number that also indicates the spirit of God manifested in matter and flesh – the natural world of living beings.

The number 5 is especially connected to human beings, as the human body has five extremities and may be outlined – with the arms and legs spread apart –

as a pentagon or five-pointed star. (Indeed, in the occult, this star represents the human being as a microcosm of the universe.)

The number 6 is characterized by harmony, equilibrium and freedom from internal strife, because it is the first number between 1 and 9 which equals the sum of its denominators: $(1 + 2 + 3 = 6)$.

The number 6 is an even and female number. However, in the same way as number 2 represents woman as the submissive contrast to dominating man, so number 6 is associated with the maternal, home-making woman: home-loving, warm, industrious, meticulous, self-satisfied and limited in her worldview.

The characteristics of peace and balance are also emphasized in the shape of the Star of David, the six-pointed star, composed of two superimposed triangles, representing equilibrium between two opposites.

On the sixth day, God created man in his image. Just as the number 5 is man's number as a microcosm of the universe, 6 is man's number as a macrocosm. It is a number that indicates the balance between spirit and matter, the eternal and the transitory. It speaks of harmony, moderation, cooperation and order.

The number 7 is the strangest and most mysterious of all numbers. Therefore, it is connected to people who delve into the occult and distance themselves from everyday life.

The number 7 appears frequently in the Bible as a symbol of wholeness and as possessing magical powers. The walls of Jericho fell after the Israelites circled them seven times; in the Book of Revelations of the New Testament, the number 7 appears numerous times.

The most prominent example of the importance of the number 7 is, of course, the days of the week – the seven days of creation, according to the Bible. The Sabbath, the day of rest, added the characteristics of quiet and withdrawal for relaxation and contemplation to the number 7.

The central characteristic of the number is its association with significant periods of time, resulting from its affinity with the moon. The lunar cycle consists of four stages of seven days each, and this division is the basis for the seven-day week and the four-week month.

Consequently, 7 is the number that controls the rhythm of life on earth, including the monthly cycle of women, upon which all human life depends. Seven objects create a unity: the planets known in antiquity numbered seven, and the number 7 corresponds with seven metals, seven colors, the seven days of the week, the seven notes of the musical scale, and the seven vowels of the Greek alphabet.

The loneliness and introversion attributed to the number 7 results from the fact that 7 is numerically a prime number.

The number 8 is twice 4, and since 4 represents earth and matter, 8 is connected with a double or emphasized interest in earthly matters – power, status and money. The concept of failure associated with the number 4 is also associated with the number 8: The constant possibility of failure is strengthened by the shape of the figure 8, hinting at a duality of success and failure.

From another viewpoint, 8 is likely to represent new beginnings and new life, perhaps since the male body has seven orifices and the female body eight – and it is through this additional eighth opening that new life comes into the world.

This fact also strengthens the connection between the number 8 and unavoidable involvement in worldly affairs. The eighth note in the musical octave repeats the first note, though an octave higher, and in the Christian numerical symbolism, the number 8 is thought to represent the afterlife and a new beginning in the world to come. Hence, the number 8 also represents eternity and infinity; the mathematical symbol for infinity is a horizontal ∞.

The two possibilities of the afterlife, eternal life in heaven as opposed to eternal life in hell, strengthen the duality concept of success and failure, which is also connected to the number 8.

The number 8 is affiliated with the primary three-dimensional body, the cube, a fact that also reinforces the connection between 8 and "new beginnings": it presents a new dimension.

The number 9 is associated with wholeness and the highest achievement, being the last number –- the highest of the first nine numbers – and the fact that human pregnancy lasts nine months. Fear of the dark, the need for love, a volatile disposition – these are all characteristics that number 9 shares with infants. Other traits, such as a desire to help others, affection and compassion, originate in the characteristics of motherhood.

The number 9 also represents the transition from single-digit numbers to double-digit numbers; in numerology, this represents intuition. It is associated with creativity, as it consists of 3 times 3.

The wholeness of number 9, as well as its self-sufficiency, is reinforced by the fact that there are 360 degrees in a circle, and that $3 + 6 + 0 = 9$. Moreover, if the numerals of each multiple of 9 are added up, they will once again result in the number 9 (for example, $3 \times 9 = 27$; $2 + 7 = 9$). Arrogance and stubbornness are also affiliated with this number.

Analyzing the Numbers

Now we will proceed to analyze numbers 1 through 9, using 12 different categories of analysis. Explanations of and elaboration on the various categories are presented at the beginning of the chapter.

1. The analysis of numbers according to the traditional approach known as "the numerology of Agricola"

The first category is the traditional analysis of people with a particular personal number. This is the traditional analysis, known in the ancient books as "the numerology of Agricola."

2. Numerological analysis according to the characteristics of love and sexuality

According to numerology, each of the nine basic numbers has a sexual characteristic. This applies when we are discussing an individual's personal number, the personal numbers of certain days – such as the days appropriate for weddings – or places, such as the hotel room number suitable for a honeymoon.

It is important to note that we only consider our own personal number or the number of the person with whom we are dealing. This number does not relate to the numbers of others, as in astrology, for example, where certain signs work well with other signs. When examining an individual's personal number as an indicator of sexuality only, we do not ask for their partner's personal number, nor is it taken into account or assessed. Numerology is indicative of the individual's sexuality, and leaves the examination of the couple's relationship to the numerological matching of partners.

Note that there is no difference or differentiation between men and women. However, it is important to remember that an individual's personal numerology, that which characterizes his behavior – including the numerology of love and sex – works in a curve-like manner. Beginning at birth, it rises sharply until the age of 21, stays at this high level, reaching its peak at 41; starts decreasing at the same rate, and at the age of 61 arrives at a point parallel to that of 21. Finally, at the age of 81, it returns to the starting point.

3. The numerological analysis of numbers according to astro-numerology, numerology that includes astrological data

Astro-numerology is the analysis of a person's qualities, character and future by means of the combination of data regarding the ruling planet and the astro-numerological birth number.

This number is solely determined by *the number of the day* in the month the individual was born.

4. Numerological analysis according to vowels

In English, there are five vowels: A, E, I, O, U. These may be interpreted through numerology, and relate mainly to the realms of the spirit, the unconscious and the soul. The way to calculate them is very simple. Write down the first and last names, mark the vowels, and add up only the numerical equivalents of the vowels so as to obtain a single-digit number.

For example: **JOHN SMITH**
Vowels: O, I
$$6 + 9 = 15 = 6$$

We will then look at what number 6 has to say about the person's spirituality.

5. Numerological analysis according to consonants

The numerology of consonants relates to the material realm (as opposed that of the vowels, which concerns spirituality). The method of calculation is similar. Write down the first and last names, mark the consonants and add them up, finally reducing the results to a single digit.

For example: **J**OHN **S**MI**TH**
Consonants: J, H, N, S, M, T, H

$$1 + 8 + 5 + 1 + 4 + 2 + 8 = 29 = 11$$

We will then have a look at the interpretation for 11 to understand the material aspect of that person's nature.

6. Numerological analysis according to the date of birth

The date of birth is the simple sum of the digits of the Gregorian birth date.

For example: 12.7.1955
$$1 + 2 + 7 + 1 + 9 + 5 + 5 = 30 = 3 + 0 = 3$$
The number of the birth date is 3.

The date of birth is a very important guide to understanding an individual's long-term behavior, both in the past as well as in the future.

7. Numerological analysis according to the birthday.

The birthday number is a special number – it predicts and directs the events of the year between one birthday and another.

Let's say that someone celebrated his 22nd birthday. In other words, he was 21 years old and became 22 years old on a certain date.

Adding 21 + 22, we get 43 = 4 + 3 = 7

Number 7 indicates what is in store for him during the coming year, between birthdays.

On his next birthday, he will go from age 22 to age 23.

22 + 23 = 45 = 4 + 5 = 9

Number 9 indicates what he may expect in the coming year, etc.

8. Numerological analysis according to the nine-year cycle

The nine-year cycle is actually a cyclical prediction for the next nine years. The difficulty always lies in determining the first year of the cycle. Once determined, we know what will occur in the years that follow.

The year is determined as described below:

Date of birth (the month and day) – reduced to a single digit, plus the year during which the inquiry is being made – reduced to a single digit, minus the thousand and hundred digits – not reduced, plus the individual's age – not reduced.

For example:

Date of birth: 12.31 = 1 + 2 + 3 + 1 = 7

Year of inquiry: 1996 = 1 + 9 + 9 + 6 = 25 = 2 + 5 = 7

Minus the thousand and hundred digits: -19

Plus the age: 26

Total: 7 + 7 + (-19) + 26 = 21 = 2 + 1 = 3

Godswill Nankey

7 6 4 1 5 933   = 6

= 3+8
= 12
2 = 3

= 8 minus 4

= 2 + 8 + 0 + 6 + 1 + 9 + 8 + 6 = 38

= 3 + 8 = 12   Henry Teigaga
                      8 55 97   25971 7
                      = 3+4   = 3+2
= 1 + 2 = 3   = 7   = 5

                      multiply 3 4 6

28 06 2018 = 26

8

annabel   nartey
1 55 1 253   5 1 925 7

= 2+2   = 2+4
= 4   = 6

Lloyd
Medina
Theo
Matthew
Francis
Me
Anike

Therefore, for the date of birth given above, 1996 will receive the number 3; 1997 – number 4; 1998 – number 5; 1999 – number 6; 2000 – number 7; 2001 – number 8; 2002 – number 9; 2003 – number 1; 2004 – number 2; 2005 – number 3.

This final number begins a new cycle of 9 years.

Note: If the total is a "minus" number, we relate to the number only and ignore the minus value.

For example:

Date of birth: 1.1

Year of inquiry: 1996

Minus the thousand and hundred digits: -19

Plus the age: 5

Total: $2 + 7 + (-19) + 5 = -5 = 5$

9. Numerological analysis according to the partnership number

When two people are married or committed to each other, their partnership number can tell us about their future.

This number is obtained by combining their personal numbers. Remember: The personal number is calculated from their first and last names prior to any change which may have taken place as a result of marriage.

For example:

SARAH PETERS

$1 + 1 + 9 + 1 + 8 + 7 + 5 + 2 + 5 + 9 + 1 = 49 = 13 = 4$

JOHN SMITH

$1 + 6 + 8 + 5 + 1 + 4 + 9 + 2 + 8 = 44 = 8$

The partnership number is $4 + 8 = 12 = 3$.

10. Numerological analysis in raising children

How can numerology be applied to raising children? How can we direct parents to concentrate on those areas in which their child needs reinforcement?

There is a simple method: From the child's date of birth, take only the day of the month. Next, add just the last digit (the unit) of the year of birth and the sun sign (astrological sign) of the child (see below) – with Aries being 1 and Pisces being 12.

For example:
Birth date: 1.25.1995.
Astrological sign: Aquarius (11)
The day: 25
The year: 5
The sign: 11
$2 + 5 + 5 + 1 + 1 = 14 = 1 + 4 = 5$
In this case, 5 is the number that will guide the child's upbringing.

Numbers corresponding with the astrological signs:

Aries – 1; Taurus – 2; Gemini – 3; Cancer – 4; Leo – 5; Virgo – 6; Libra – 7; Scorpio – 8; Sagittarius – 9; Capricorn – 10; Aquarius – 11; Pisces – 12.

11. Numerological analysis according to first and last names

The number corresponding to one's name is obtained by adding all the letters of the first and last names, resulting in one numerological number. The first and last names are written down, then the numerical values of the letters are added up and reduced to one digit.

For example: **JOHN SMITH**

$$1 + 6 + 8 + 5 + 1 + 4 + 9 + 2 + 8 = 44 = 4 + 4 = 8$$

This is the number corresponding to John Smith's name. We then look at the number 8 and see what it means.

12. Numerological analysis according to cosmic vibrations

When we talk about the basic form of numbers, we are referring to their inherent cosmic vibrations. Every number contains a particular characteristic cosmic vibration that distinguishes it from the other numbers.

This idea can help us follow the train of thought of philosophers such as Pythagoras and Agrippa who related to the universe as if it were a vibrating being.

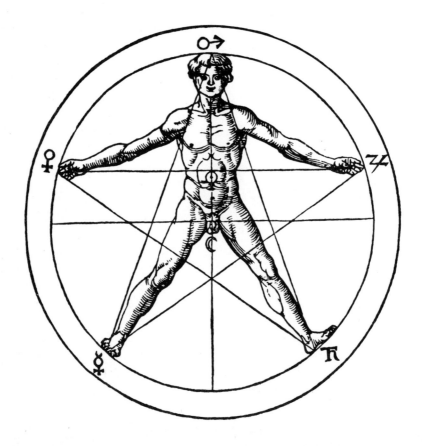

Number *1*

1. The numerological analysis of number 1 according to the traditional

approach known as "the numerology of Agricola"

Number 1 people are self-confident, active and daring. They are the researchers, the pioneers, the explorers, who are gifted with a scientist's curiosity and an artist's creative imagination. They are intelligent, logical, decisive and domineering - albeit in a pleasant way. Their ambitiousness and initiative frequently elevate them to positions of power and authority. These individuals know exactly what they want and stick to their goal: *One always remains one*, identical to himself, despite any separation or division. They have no need for advice and encouragement from others, and it is very difficult to divert them from their chosen path. They are creative, original, born leaders, brave, and effective in emergencies. They know how to control their feelings and operate with speed and concentration. They are vital and full of energy, are able to overcome any adversary, and suffer pain and tribulation without complaint. They can adjust to the most dire circumstances and will never shirk a task or responsibility.

Although they are, on occasion, eccentric, violent, impatient, intolerant and stubborn, they usually enjoy a good deal of popularity and admiration. They are generous and forgiving, and always show sympathy for the weak and helpless.

Number 1 people feel a great responsibility toward their loved ones, and are not particularly jealous. However, if they are hurt by a show of blatant infidelity, they are liable to be merciless in their rage.

They enjoy homes that are managed prudently. They are thrifty and never slip into blatant overspending, although they are generous toward their partners.

Number 1 people are logical and always willing to compromise. They never carry on fighting if it is at all possible to end it peacefully. They are charming, attractive, affectionate and honest people.

One signifies the Creator of the universe, the number of God. In addition, the number 1 represents masculinity and power. Just as every number divided by one remains itself, so the spirit of a number 1 person is able to pass through many different situations and transformations without changing its essence.

2. The numerological analysis of number 1 according to characteristics of love and sexuality

The shape of number 1 in itself indicates that this group aims for fulfillment in sex. For them, love that is unfulfilled is not perfect (and note once again that there is no difference between men and women). The actualization of love and sex always demands some degree of penetration into their partner's personal space. There is no manifestation of love when number 1 remains alone.

Consequently, logic, discretion and social norms dictate number 1's sexuality. In a relationship, emotional considerations are relegated to second place. In other words, if we desire to characterize number 1's sexuality, we turn to the conventions and norms in his social environment. This regards lifestyle as well as the timetable according to which each thing occurs.

Number 1 people are very physical in their love and must go through all the motions in order to feel that they are "OK". This does not only apply to penetration, the main factor in number 1's sexuality.

Their love is sensual, and it is difficult to find a number 1 who settles for platonic love. At a young age, their love is expressed by curiosity and an attempt to fulfill their sexuality. However, following a certain stabilization, their sexuality declines. Because love and sexuality are connected to physical fulfillment for number 1 people, this hits them hard at an older age: "If it's not physical, it's not love!"

3. The numerological analysis of number 1 according to astro-numerology

For this purpose, number 1 people are those born on the first, tenth, nineteenth or twenty-eighth day of the month.

(Individuals born under the sign of Capricorn also have tendencies related to number 1, but for astrological purposes they are not included here. The same applies to people for whom the sum of the letters of their name equals 1. In both those cases, we are discussing numerology and not astro-numerology. This also applies to all other basic numbers in the following astro-numerological analysis.)

The sun is the symbol of light, of primary energy. The astrological symbol of the sun - a point within a circle - symbolizes the cyclical nature of infinity. Each point on the circle is equidistant from the center, and the circumference does not possess a defined beginning or end.

The central point is actually the source and beginning of all things, the origin of light, of life, and of the expression of God's might.

We sometimes see the sun identified with God, and in polytheistic cultures, it is identified with the principal god.

It is important to grasp that human beings consider the sun as setting the rhythm of day and night, darkness and light. The sun also determines the Divine Trinity: sunrise (birth), the movement of the sun across the sky (life), and sunset (death). (This is one of the sources for the Holy Trinity in Christianity, or the trinity of gods in Hinduism: Brahma, Vishnu and Shiva.)

The sun gives life to everything, and is at the foundation of all creation. The sun gives human beings their spark, their uniqueness, and connects them to God.

In addition, the sun is the center of the solar system, and illuminates the moon.

Traditionally, the sun is the male principle, indicating a warm character and an active, passionate sexuality.

The sun is represented as movement along a straight line, bursting forth, like number 1. It is an eruptive and creative force.

Most important is the relationship between the sun and the moon, the two great luminaries. Likewise, the two most influential basic numbers in numerology are number 1 – the number of the sun, and number 2 – that of the moon.

4. The numerological analysis of number 1 according to vowels

This indicates excellent abilities as a leader of the masses. You are ambitious and always aspire to succeed and race forward. This even permits you to push others around and elbow your way roughly.

You are original, innovative and uncompromising when it comes to quality. You are able to be independent and not take your talents for granted, but rather to hone them to excellence.

You tend not to listen to the advice of friends or others around you if you are uncertain of their intentions. While you are creative, you have an exaggerated degree of self-assurance. If you really wish to go far, you must keep the arrogant side of your nature in check and treat others with humility and respect.

The lack of patience that you occasionally display is liable to be a hindrance to you. You must learn to be more perceptive under certain circumstances, so as not to cause embarrassment to those around you. Being involved in public activities or politics would help you to develop the tact and manners of a diplomat.

5. The numerological analysis of number 1 according to consonants

You are domineering. Although you are gifted with organizational and managerial skills and know how to get the most out of a team of workers, you occasionally achieve this in a rude and ruthless manner. Learn to use a more gentle approach. Sometimes, giving orders is not the best way to achieve an objective, since your subordinates will carry out your demands not out of desire or love, but because they have no choice.

Learn to channel your energy in positive directions. It will enable you to get the most out of yourself and out of the organization or staff that you head. Your managerial talents are noteworthy and your appearance inspires respect. You enjoy looking different than other people, although it seems as if you are afraid of this tendency. It is possible that over the years you have encountered cynicism, which has engendered your fear. However, you must be open to the world and cultivate a stronger trust in others – it will enable you to give and receive more love.

6. The numerological analysis of number 1 according to the date of birth

The struggle to reach your goals and objectives never ends. As soon as you overcome one, another one immediately presents itself.

The type of decisions you make determines the results. The general direction is toward an expression of your inner self and your organizational and leadership abilities. It is important to depend on your unique talents and skills, and always to aim for the best, most successful results.

7. The numerological analysis of number 1 according to the birthday

This may indicate that you are about to adopt a new position or take courses of action different than those you normally take. Keeping an open and flexible mind will help you immensely during this period of life. If you accept changes in life positively, it will help you adjust more easily to new situations. You must be aware of your state of health; it is possible that certain changes will affect your general health in the future. Be aware of the signals your body sends you and do not neglect them.

This is an excellent period for meeting new people who will bring you genuine friendship. Listen carefully to your intuitive feelings and follow your heart.

You can expect success at work. This is a good time, as there is the possibility of promotion or, on the other hand, of handsome profits. Family life may suffer. Invest more energy in domestic relationships and devote more attention to those who are particularly dear to you.

8. The numerological analysis of number 1 according to the nine-year cycle

A good year! This is the time to broaden your knowledge in areas you always wanted to explore but never did. You now prefer to sever ties with people who limit you or hold you back.

You are more than ever willing to try new things and you are open to new ideas. Take advantage of your developing sense of boldness and desire for innovation.

If until now earthly things distracted you and prevented you from engaging in inner contemplation, this is the time to devote time to yourself. Re-familiarize yourself with different aspects of your personality and get to know the ins and outs of your soul and your inner world, which have been neglected until now.

9. The numerological analysis of number 1 according to the

partnership number

The partners must be clear about each other's limits, and learn not to impinge on the other's territory or personal space. Each one must respect the other's wish for privacy. They have very different personalities and fields of interest; this means that they are two individualists who, if they are squeezed together, might go their separate ways for good. If each one learns to respect the other's desire for true freedom, there is a greater chance that this partnership will last. Each must exercise a certain degree of self-control and practice restraint – even when this is very difficult or when he/she feels deprived of their partner's attention.

10. The numerological analysis of number 1 in raising children

The general development of the child should be guided by freedom of choice. Encourage him in his attempts to experience new things. Reinforce his desire to include others and be an integrated, open individual. Help him develop his ability to be self-critical and to judge things objectively.

An approach that is too rigid will destroy his ability to be independent and make choices on his own. Give him freedom of choice and ample room to move, not limiting or stifling his actions. The more supportive his environment, the more balanced his fundamental characteristics will be.

If the child is given the opportunity to experience different things and face challenges on his own, he will develop self-confidence and will not be dependent on others. A child who is aware of danger will know how to take care of himself. His parents must remember that each child has to experiment on his own and learn to avoid mistakes through his own personal experience.

Even if he is aware of the failures of others, he will not always be careful until he has actually learned from his own experience. This is the way of the world, and parents must be aware of this and not force their opinions or authority on the child – an approach that might produce the opposite results.

11. The numerological analysis of number 1 according to the first and

last name

You constantly aspire to express your personality in every original way possible. This is the epitome of your life's aspirations and objectives – to let your desires and ambitions run free, unfettered by society's mores and constraints.

You love privacy, and preserving it takes top priority in your life. If you really do desire to fulfill this ambition, you will be compelled to take responsibility for your life and not compromise. You will have to be sufficiently courageous to deal with the many obstacles in your path. Only after a difficult struggle will you reach your objective.

You enjoy being a pioneer in various fields and investigating new ideas. The pursuit of challenges and reaching the goals you have set for yourself in life cause the adrenaline to flow in your body. Every once in a while, you need to experience success as proof of your actions. It gives you satisfaction and encourages you to work toward the next objective.

12. The numerological analysis of number 1 according to cosmic vibrations

The number 1 represents the primal and primeval component that was created from infinity (that is, from 0).

It is extremely difficult to discuss the number 1 because it is a prime number, single and solitary. This means that if there is no other number with it, it is impossible to compare it to anything else.

Since human thought can only analyze reality on a comparative basis, and since the number 1 does not afford such a basis, all we can say about it is that it exists.

The number 1 is represented by a dot in the center of a circle or by a single line.

Number 2

1. The numerological analysis of number 2 according to the traditional approach known as "the numerology of Agricola"

Number 2 people are creative and sensitive, and have a highly developed imagination. They are reserved, but stand up for themselves, and are likely to be brilliant writers, artists, musicians, and teachers.

They are not born leaders; most prefer to play a secondary role. But, at the same time, since they are resourceful and open to new ideas, they are able to be clever and modest employees. They are usually wonderful conversationalists, very witty and are gifted with a full-blown sense of humor. They are gifted with a highly developed intuition and many have extrasensory perception (ESP). Number 2 people are quiet, tactful, and easy-going. They abhor anger and conflict, and love beauty, harmony, and order.

They are able to adjust easily and gracefully to changing circumstances, but if their emotional or financial security is jeopardized, they are liable to become extremely depressed, to the point of physical illness. They have a particular tendency toward ulcers and digestive problems. Number 2 people are moody and may suffer from melancholy, resulting largely from imaginary fears. An unpleasant comment in passing or a strange look is liable to offend them deeply, and cause them to withdraw and cloak themselves in an accusing blanket of silence.

Usually, they possess a pleasant and friendly temperament. However, like the moon, they have a dark side; they can be intolerant, hypercritical and possessive. They are generally shy and introverted, and do not like to make decisions, changing their minds frequently.

They tend to dwell on their mistakes, and often suffer feelings of incompleteness, disadvantage and dissatisfaction with themselves.

As spouses, they are faithful and loving, but tend to be jealous, even about insignificant things. They require reinforcement, encouragement, and constant displays of love, and are willing to bestow love and encouragement in return. They tend to compromise, and will always be happy to stop fighting and make up. They love a comfortable home, are good and devoted parents, and are careful when it comes to spending money.

Number 2 people are cautious with money, and need the security of savings in case of emergency. They are likely to feel economically insecure even if objectively there is no reason for concern. They are sociable, popular and admired at times.

Number 2 symbolizes duality, male and female, negative and positive, conscious and unconscious, good and evil. It is also considered a symbol of femininity, receptiveness, passivity, and motherhood.

2. The numerological analysis of number 2 according to characteristics of

love and sexuality

Many numerologists make the mistake of viewing number 2 people's sexuality as a continuation of that of number 1. One is active, the other passive, one bursts forward, the other receives. These numerologists would do well to review the sources once again. Their assessments concerning the delicate subject of love and sexuality are incorrect and misleading.

Actually, the sexuality of a number 2 person should be viewed as consisting of *two* number 1s standing back to back.

And what does this mean?

Number 2 has a healthy sexual appetite for variation, change and innovation, as opposed to the constant repetition of known and familiar routines.

Number 2 people are conscious of the fact that their sexuality and way of loving is a "given", but are also aware that love and sexual relationships result from interaction between couples. The more they vary and change partners, the more they discover additional aspects of their sexuality.

As a result, they are constantly searching for new and preferably different partners. The image of "two number 1s standing back to back" indicates that number 2s are consistently seeking opportunities for love and sex, and therefore have a reputation for promiscuity.

On the other hand, the degree of variation in their relationships does not necessarily promise especially good sexual relations. Regarding love, it may present an obstacle larger than any possible advantage. Moreover, number 2's love does not stem from the depths of an emotional wellspring - it is based mainly on urges that are fulfilled with the help of logic. This logical thinking teaches number 2 people that the fulfillment of urges is a way of life for them.

3. The numerological analysis of number 2 according to astro-numerology

This refers to those born on the second, eleventh, twentieth and twenty-ninth of the month.

The main characteristic of the moon is that it reflects the light and warmth of the sun, and transfers that light to the realm of night and darkness. Therefore, the moon represents the unconscious mind, internal feeling and human instinct.

Anything that is unable to penetrate a person's armor during daylight infiltrates the depths of the unconscious at night by means of dreams that are governed by the moonlight.

The popular symbol of the moon is the crescent, a semicircle that absorbs and reflects the sun's light. But we must remember that when there is an eclipse of the moon, a circle with a crescent within it is formed: This is the symbol of perfect divinity, containing both the male and the female. In other words, the moon is complementary to, as well as the entirety of, the sun. This concept is likewise expressed in the well-known symbol of *yin* and *yang*.

The moon represents the female aspect of God, or the goddess who rules the heavens side by side with the sun god.

Although number 2 is second to number 1, and represents the feminine, passive, absorbing, and nurturing principle, we must remember that in many cultures it is specifically this principle which rules. For ultimately, it was woman alone - the moon - who had the ability to ensure the continuation of a royal dynasty.

Number 2, like the moon, determines and implants emotions in the unconscious mind. Hence, it is the connection with the past and with the basic body of subconscious human knowledge. And it is this number that determines feelings, impulses and passions, and particularly all processes connected to birth and death.

It is important to understand that while number 1, the sun, is too direct and powerful for human beings to experience firsthand, the moon filters that power and transfers it to us in smaller, steady doses. Therefore, in most cases, the moon's influence is likely to be much stronger than that of the sun.

The moon, number 2, is the most important factor in shaping character, social adjustment, and family life.

The relationship between the sun and the moon is the cornerstone of the horoscope and the birth chart.

On the numerological chart, number 2 is no less significant than number 1. We must remember that the combination of 1 + 2 allows us to be creative. Giving and receiving bring about new creation.

4. The numerological analysis of number 2 according to vowels

You must be more assertive. You tend to agree with those around you and accept things even if you are not totally satisfied with them and would actually like to change them. You *can* do that; gifted with highly developed senses and awareness of what is going on around you, you are also able to discern subtleties. You are very tactful and have excellent diplomatic skills.

If it were up to you, the world would consist of nirvana alone.

It would not hurt if you developed a thicker skin to protect yourself from insults and offensive comments that are hard for you to take. If you found a way to cope with this kind of aggressiveness, you would no doubt be a happier person. You are very strong emotionally. People like you are the least likely to have a mental breakdown.

At times, you feel that you have the ability to lead the entire world. But this is not really so! Despite your spiritual abilities, your vulnerability does not permit it. It is preferable for you to follow other people's orders rather than aspire to leadership; in this way, you will be spared unnecessary suffering. You do not have the strength to stand up to the conflicts that this struggle involves.

You have the makings of a medium. The intensity of these traits may be frightening at times, but you must learn to use them for your own benefit and take maximum advantage of them.

5. The numerological analysis of number 2 according to consonants

You are a very pleasant person. You are not aggressive and even if at times you express some aggressiveness, it is never vociferous and never takes the form of incomprehensible outbursts.

You exude pleasantness and amiability. People enjoy being in your presence.

You will never attack those around you nor will you take advantage of someone else's weakness. You are extremely tactful. Thanks to these qualities, it is very easy for you to make friends, and you are always surrounded by people. While preferring to stay in the background and not stand out, you certainly have a lot to say and have definite opinions.

You enjoy voicing these opinions and are aware of your intelligence. However, you will always find the right moment to speak your mind without being overly conspicuous and without causing provocation. See that you always preserve your uniqueness, as you usually succeed in doing.

You are not good at pretense. However, if you do not like someone, you will invariably hide your feelings and avoid him elegantly. On occasion, your sincerity lands you in embarrassing situations. However, if you stick to your own path – the one you usually follow, you may be sure it is the correct one.

6. The numerological analysis of number 2 according to the date of birth

Your desire is to live among a close-knit group of people. Your need to assimilate and mix with others allows you to cooperate well with them, and this will bring positive opportunities in the future.

Life teaches us to compromise. At times, it is necessary to let others take center stage and allow them to progress while you stand in the wings. Rely on those who are capable of giving you unbounded and unconditional love and support.

You have the natural ability to survive in difficult and uncomfortable conditions, and are extremely adaptable. You do not pursue status or esteem, and in general, although you do not seek prestige, you will obtain it as a result of your natural leadership qualities.

You have a tendency to be dragged into situations that encourage dependence and an inability to control your destiny and be your own boss. You are then deprived of the ability to think for yourself and act freely.

7. The numerological analysis of number 2 according to the birthday

This indicates a change in location. Number 2 points to partnerships, either in your business or in your personal life, and may occur during times of economic difficulty or emotional blocks. You tend to be a good listener. During this period, you are not taking care of yourself as you usually do. You tend to invest a lot of effort in hard work, going into great detail. Focusing on peripheral things may prove destructive. It may also come at the expense of more significant things in life. Control your tendency to be a perfectionist. Unwittingly, you are neglecting other things that are significant to your future. This time of pressure will soon pass, so do not allow yourself to sink into depression or despair, even if your present situation appears bleak. You may depend on your partner. Get rid of some of the burden of responsibility you are carrying on your shoulders and you will discover that the resulting relief will influence your entire being.

8. The numerological analysis of number 2 according to the nine-year cycle

By the end of the year, you hope to reach a much higher point than where you started at the beginning of the year. It is important to you not to get stuck in a rut. You do not settle for simply maintaining the status quo. This strong, relentless desire to reach higher levels and greater achievements in life will accompany you throughout the year. You are liable to experience great disappointment if in the final reckoning you feel that you did not succeed in attaining the objectives you set for yourself at the beginning of the year.

9. The numerological analysis of number 2 according to the

partnership number

Both partners must work hard at cooperating. Without this cooperation, the partnership will not survive. They must be patient and understanding with each other during times of crisis, and must learn to live in harmony. Momentary outbursts must not be allowed to cause rifts in the relationship. They must beware of getting involved in a power struggle. The more they cooperate with and listen to each other, the more successful their life together will be.

10. The numerological analysis of number 2 in raising children

The number 2 child is highly sensitive and needs a lot of help. He faces life hesitatantly and imagines that it is full of danger. Life seems threatening and parents must do their best to give him a secure, solid base. He will find it easier to cope with the early years of life if he is in a warm familiar environment, surrounded by things he loves that are soothing and make him happy.

The number 2 child likes drifting off into the world of the imagination. His imaginary experiences are so realistic to him that at times he loses himself in the stories he has made up. His parents must help him set boundaries between imagination and reality, and know when to put an end to his daydreaming and bring him back to earth. They are responsible for the child's mental well-being. Their child is very sensitive and they must be conscious of any change in his personality or any display of weakness or fear. Children do not explain themselves or their inner world very well. If the parents are not alert and do not identify problems in time to nip them in the bud, they run the risk of causing unintentional emotional damage that will take a long time to repair later on.

11. The numerological analysis of number 2 according to the first and

last name

You are a person with a special sensitivity to others and to your surroundings. If you are to choose a vocation, social work, psychology or counseling would be good choices. There is no doubt that you would be very successful in these fields.

You are gifted with an extraordinary ability to listen to the needs of others and be aware of their distress and sensitive to their desires. You are very patient and possess the sincere empathy and great love needed to understand others. Your intuitive abilities help you to comprehend other people's feelings and assist them.

You are overflowing with warmth and are able to give a lot of love to those around you. You always offer people warmth and sensitivity, as well as a shoulder to cry on. While you enjoy delicate and sensitive things, rudeness and coarse behavior offend you.

12. The numerological analysis of number 2 according to cosmic vibrations

The number 2 represents duality and separation in their potential form. With the creation of this number, values such as "I" as opposed to "you" came into being. Again, we are not talking about holistic existence (represented by 0) or a single number (represented by 1) – but rather about a split and the consequent breakdown of unity.

The number 2 is represented and symbolized by two horizontal lines: = , which became Z over the years, and finally 2.

Number *3*

1. The numerological analysis of number 3 according to the traditional approach known as "the numerology of Agricola"

Number 3 people are clever, crafty, and alert, with original ideas. They usually are one step ahead of everyone else. They are creative, artistic, reliable and refined. Number 3 signifies a trinity, the number of enlightenment, and indicates sympathy and intuition. Number 3 people are likely to be brilliant scientists, statesmen, writers and painters. They are multifaceted and quick-thinking, always triumph in verbal duels, have a penchant for satire, and occasionally enjoy making fun of people who think more slowly than they do.

They are capable of concentrating on several things at one time and absorbing the main ideas of a book, for example, just by leafing through it briefly. They have a highly developed sense of order and justice and are ready to submit to discipline and limitations to a certain extent, but can also be stubborn, and even domineering. At times, they speak too bluntly, and may therefore be misunderstood. In actual fact, they do not have a malicious bone in their bodies, and would be appalled by the idea that a tactless comment on their part embarrassed or offended another person. They are easy-going and make friends easily, but may flare up suddenly if they think someone is trying to take advantage of them. Although they are independent and proud, they consider it important to know what others think of them.

They are especially fortunate; a seemingly disastrous event is likely to be a blessing in disguise and will bring them happiness.

In love, they are very loyal and consistent; they radiate warmth, but are impulsive. They are not particularly jealous or possessive. They love nature and beautiful scenery and manage quite well in a house that is not quite up to par. Their relationship with their partner is more important than any other. They are not especially interested in money, are likely to be very generous to the ones they like, and are always willing to compromise.

Number 3 symbolizes the union of negative and positive, which together create a new situation. It represents the affinity between contrasts – a man and a woman conceiving a child. The tendency to connect number 3 with loftiness goes back to antiquity. The Pythagoreans referred to this number as the "perfect number" because it has a beginning, a middle and an end. There is a belief that the number 3 has a mystical meaning. Greek mythology tells about the Three Graces. Neptune carries a trident as his identifying symbol and the Oracle at Delphi stood before a tripod. Spells and oaths are usually repeated three times. The number 3 also appears frequently in legends: There are three wishes, three guesses or three riddles.

2. The numerological analysis of number 3 according to characteristics of love and sexuality

Enter emotions! Number 3 people bring feelings into the picture. And this should not be underestimated. These people exhibit a very strong sexuality along with devoted long-term love.

Many view those whose number is three as the first who will achieve a couple relationship, according to the premise that "it takes two to tango." This saying contains a great deal of numerological truth, resulting from the general traits of number 3.

Number 3 indicates a brand of love and sexuality expressed with a great degree of intensity – very passionate, but also consistent over a long period of time.

Although this does not necessarily ensure the quality of the relationship, in most cases, the quantity and intensity are sufficient in themselves. Therefore, number 3 people are considered to have good, and even more important, stable sexuality and love.

It is significant that number 3 people love with emotion, which serves as the glue that preserves love through the passage of time.

For example, these individuals do not exhibit a decline in their ability to love during the latter part of their lives.

There is no doubt that, as a serious partner, number 3 has a certain advantage over number 1 or 2.

However, before choosing a partner, consider the rest of the numbers.

3. The numerological analysis of number 3 according to astro-numerology

This refers to those born on the third, twelfth, twenty-first or thirtieth day of the month.

Number 3 as it appears in the symbol of Jupiter contains the symbol of the absorbing moon together with a cross. It is like number 1, but on different planes of vertical and horizontal. In other words, it is a combination of spirit and matter, capable of bringing about new creation.

Number 3 is the number that unites the male and the female forces and introduces new creativity into the material world. To a degree, this is also true of the nature of the planet Jupiter, a planet whose mythological symbol pursues human females and spreads his progeny over the earth!

Jupiter demands that the individual combine his physical, material ability with his spiritual ability in order to ascend to the loftiest peaks of the universe. Jupiter also shows him the way, and there is no doubt that Jupiter's Hebrew name, Zedek (justice), reflects his nature.

Number 3 is a key number in any numerological analysis. The ultimate aim of the numerological chart is to provide practical guidelines for one's life, and number 3 points the individual in the right direction and illuminates his path.

4. The numerological analysis of number 3 according to vowels

You are the kind of person who always gets along. Wherever you are, you invariably make friends and find yourself at the center of attention.

You are gifted with extraordinary acting abilities and excellent writing skills. You love company and will always be the life and soul of the party. You enjoy parties and social gatherings. Since you are always socially prominent and find yourself at the center of things, people invariably seek your company and want to be close to you. You know how to tell jokes and say the right thing at the right time. Other people never feel embarrassed in your presence, and you have the ability to make anyone – even someone you have just met – feel comfortable.

You are full of *joie de vivre* and cordiality. It is easy for those around you to be caught up in your cheerful mood.

However, you are impulsive and must learn to control your desires and wishes of the moment. This is not always easy. If the number 3 is the sum of the vowels in your name, you must learn to concentrate on one thing rather than spreading yourself thinly over many areas.

5. The numerological analysis of number 3 according to consonants

You are sociable and friendly, abounding with charm. People seek your company and especially want to be seen in your presence. You look great. Every color and fashion suits you. At any social event, you immediately become the center of attention. There is no doubt that you know how to take advantage of this situation, and make sure it brings small perks. You are particularly optimistic and view your life as lucky. You are quite hedonistic and enjoy the good life – fine dining, elegant night spots, and getting the most out of life. You love comfort and are definitely not one to go on long treks or sleep outside in a sleeping-bag.

Usually, you know exactly what suits you and how to plan your actions. Leaving things unresolved or unfinished bothers you, and it can be said that you aspire to perfection. At the same time, you do not demand the same degree of perfectionism from others, and this may be one of the secrets of your success and popularity amongst those around you.

From the negative point of view, you expect immediate gratification; if you do not get it, you act childishly.

6. The numerological analysis of number 3 according to the date of birth

You are offered many opportunities for working in different fields, particularly the arts. There are possibilities of achieving a level of spiritual wholeness and joy. The general direction points to freedom, the legitimization of different modes of expression, and release from narrow, limited thinking; there are also broadened horizons and openness resulting from the development of consciousness. You should avoid extreme actions, as they do not suit your personality. It is also advisable to exercise restraint and not to tempt fate. Taking the wrong turn may lead to uneasiness and consequently to a loss of self-confidence. It is worthwhile to be organized even if it is incompatible with your desire to be spontaneous and act according to your feelings. If something requires advance planning, making a list or a daily schedule, do it! Avoid unnecessary confusion that might impair your development. Structure, organization, order and planning will prevent you from landing up in difficult situations that will lead to undesirable results.

7. The numerological analysis of number 3 according to the birthday

This indicates a desire to be at the center of things – to influence and lead – and it is possible that this desire will affect your distant future. This is a good time to establish relationships and acquire a high position in the company or institution with which you are affiliated. If you are not drawn to public activity, you may need to channel your energies elsewhere. Number 3 indicates artistic activity and the revealing of previously hidden skills. This is the time to publicize your work. Your self-confidence is stronger than it has ever been. You are able to withstand criticism. Do not hesitate to display your talents; it might pay off in the end and generate financial benefits.

This is a good period for professional development. Do not be tempted to stop studying in favor of something that may appear promising at the moment. Your studies will give you a significant boost in the future.

8. The numerological analysis of number 3 according to the nine-year cycle

This is a positive year that will bring you great happiness. However, you must seek it. If you sit back and wait, there is no certainty that you will reap all the benefits that this year may bring. You may experience things you did not even dream of experiencing. Achievements will follow the hard work and efforts of previous years. You will finally reap the fruits of your labor, and the rewards will be greater than you ever imagined. You will always be in the right place at the right time, and have your cake and eat it too! The timing of surprises will always be in your favor. Take full advantage of this situation.

Do not hesitate to express yourself and your ideas. Muster your self-confidence. Your ideas will be granted renewed validity, and your friends will hold you in higher esteem than ever.

Your inner freedom and sense of release are intoxicating. Do not be tempted to be swept away by these feelings. Restrain yourself and set limits so that you will not find yourself leaping from one extreme to the next. Go with the flow and let yourself be led to new discoveries of yourself and of others.

This year is one of new beginnings in various areas affecting your future. Far-reaching changes may come your way this year, perhaps even unexpectedly, without prior warning.

For public servants, this will be a year of public recognition. Finally, after years of effort and hard work, you will reap the fruits of your labor. Success will be far-reaching, and surprisingly so. The more careful you are with the social side of things, the greater your success will be.

Even during difficult times, you must maintain high morale and good spirits. It will help you overcome crises and influence your immediate surroundings. The more restraint you display, not allowing your spirits to fall, the more those around you will hold you in high esteem.

9. The numerological analysis of number 3 according to the partnership number

Difficulties in communication may undermine even a relationship based on love. The partners must learn to express themselves, whether for solving problems and releasing pressure verbally, or for sharing their feelings of love and affection verbally – not only physically.

Good and open communication is a vital basis for the relationship. The partners must learn to share their experiences and tell each other what is going on in their hearts and souls. It is important to know how to express joy and not be repressed or restrained. The better they are at sharing and expressing joyful experiences, the more complete and rewarding their lives will be.

10. The numerological analysis of number 3 in raising children

The number 3 child is extraordinarily active. Parents must take a lot of trouble with him in order to ensure that he has outlets for his temperament.

If the parents are careful, they will be able to achieve several objectives at once: develop the child's imagination and thought processes, and enable him to release his inner energy via positive channels. The minute the parents let up, the child is liable to lose control completely.

If active children are given due attention and taught to channel their energy in positive ways, they can become the type of adults who make a contribution to society, often assuming leadership roles in which they are heeded and followed by many people.

The number 3 child needs a tremendous amount of warmth and love. He externalizes his emotions, and if he doesn't receive the attention he requires, he demands it in other ways.

He likes to use his imagination and play "make believe." He divides his world into clear categories of "good guys" and "bad guys." He is stubborn, and it is hard to get him to obey. Parents must learn to cope with his disobedience gently, and not in an authoritarian manner that will make him more aggressive and cause him to display violent behavior patterns.

11. The numerological analysis of number 3 according to the first and

last name

You are essentially an actor. Gifted with theatrical talent, you love to perform in front of an audience and make them feel happy and uplifted. You enjoy making people laugh, thus providing them with an outlet for their tensions. Your talents manifest themselves in your verbal abilities and writing skills. If you combine your talents properly, you will benefit from all the facets of your personality.

Since you know how to entertain people and make them laugh, you could be a successful stand-up comedian. Every now and then, your ability to entertain and amuse enables you to extricate yourself gracefully from embarrassing situations.

Your ability to cause happiness, enjoyment and laughter is a source of much joy to you. You derive a lot of satisfaction from the fact that you are able to give of yourself to others. It may fill your life completely. Be careful not to spread your talents too thinly.

At times, you become too involved in your theatrical world. You may forget to be attentive enough to your family, focusing instead on your colleagues or other people. Avoid having too many fingers in too many pies, and do not let your attention stray from the most important things.

In spite of your acting talents and your ability to don masks without others being aware of it, you are honest and open by nature. You are able tell those close to you what you think of them – even if it is unpleasant.

Try to tone down your manner, since every now and then you are liable to offend someone unintentionally. Attempt to channel the talents you have been blessed with in positive directions that will be uplifting to others.

12. The numerological analysis of number 3 according to cosmic vibrations

The number 3 represents the formation of the plane, that is of space. The creation of this number gives reality relativity. The number 3 contributed the second dimension to the universe and created area. From now on, both length and breadth exist.

The number 3 brought plane, space, relativity, and area into being, but it is also a primary number that exists without matter. On the basis of these three points, it is not possible to create a shape with volume, and without this, there is no matter!

The number 3 is represented and symbolized by means of a triangle: △ , or by means of three horizontal lines which gradually became 3.

Number 4

1. The numerological analysis of number 4 according to the traditional approach known as "the numerology of Agricola"

Number 4 people are vigorous, energetic and idealistic, willing to work hard and likely to be good managers. They are very practical, and many are, indeed, involved in the administrative aspects of business. They are very happy when they can work for others, and have a strong desire to fight poverty and suffering in order to make the world a better place. Thanks to their common sense and outstanding organizational skills, they are likely to be extremely effective in institutions of charity and working for the general good. They may be very successful in choosing a profession and career. However, they generally achieve status and establish themselves only after a lot of hard work. They are occasionally jealous of those who surpass them professionally, despite the fact that they did not work as hard.

Number 4 people excel as scientists, inventors, painters, writers, musicians, architects, builders, farmers, secretaries and stage directors. Although they may appear slightly eccentric, these people are productive, decisive, punctual, and very reliable. They are good conversationalists, and their comments are often thought-provoking; they minds are full of original and unusual ideas.

Their laughter is usually contagious, and they love to hear and tell amusing stories. They do not seek attention, but are capable of getting it if they so desire. Their lives are varied, action-packed and filled to the brim with interesting events and happenings. They are sensitive, patriotic, home-loving and highly self-disciplined.

When it comes to love they are sentimental, loyal and considerate, but not particularly jealous. They usually have a large circle of friends but prefer the company of their partner. Family life is very important to them. In spite of their caution regarding money matters, they are quite generous with their partner and are willing to sacrifice anything for her or him. They try to live peacefully with their relatives, detest quarrels, and are gifted with the skills of diplomacy.

Four is the number of solid matter and is especially connected to the earth. The symbol of this form is the square or the cube, representing stability, materialism and physical strength. According to ancient and medieval beliefs, everything in the world is composed of different combinations of the four elements: earth, air, fire and water, in different states of wetness, dryness, heat, and cold, and exist above and beyond each individual element.

There are four levels of the self: the physical body, the astral body, the soul, and the spirit. There are four functions: sensing, feeling, thinking and intuition. There are four forms of matter: minerals, gases, plants and animals.

2. The numerological analysis of number 4 according to characteristics of love and sexuality and sexuality

Number 4 people are universally known as squares. However, this definition alone is not sufficient in the area of sexuality and love. In fact, this definition does them an injustice.

The principal trait of number 4 people is that they are "slow and thorough" in love. They take their time and are not rapidly seduced (and do not let go quickly, either). Their love and sexuality develop slowly, and are based on a balance between emotions and physicality, between passion and love.

Furthermore, in order to bond with another, they must first be convinced that both logically and emotionally they are doing exactly the right thing.

Hence, the stage of considering and examining, groping and feeling one's way, is the longest and most significant period in number 4's sexuality. The slow development of the relationship deters potential partners at times.

However, as soon as the connection is indeed forged – all factors considered and all con-clusions reached – number 4's love may then express itself fully.

At this stage, people with number 4 exhibit a strong, fundamental and ongoing sexuality, with a love that is balanced, sincere, and long-lasting. There is no doubt that after the stage of feeling their way, and despite the label of "square", number 4 people reveal a stable and beautiful side of sexuality and love.

3. The numerological analysis of number 4 according to astro-numerology

This refers to those born on the fourth, thirteenth, twenty-second or thirty-first day of the month.

Uranus is the planet on the birth chart that is mostly sensed when in an unfavorable position! It might be said that Uranus rules the sixth sense, human intuition. Beyond the senses, beyond the understanding of number 1 aided by number 2 in order to activate number 3, human beings need intuition in order to make their way through life.

And in this case, intuition is obtained by number 4 using the astrological approach (as opposed to the trait associated with number 4 when analyzed as a number). We might say that when Uranus is in a good position in the birth chart, it allows one to preserve his identity while at the same time assimilating into his surroundings. Perhaps that is the essence of number 4's material foundation!

When the number 4 is missing from a numerological chart, the individual in question is greatly dependent on others, particularly with respect to choosing his path in life. Number 4 (Uranus) is crucial if one wants to go up to a new and higher plane in life.

4. The numerological analysis of number 4 according to vowels

You have both feet firmly planted on the ground and are very realistic. You are able to see reality as it is without needing to embellish it. Anything that does not directly contribute to the cause is unimportant in your eyes. You are responsible and may be trusted implicitly.

You can be given authority without hesitation. You stick to the task at hand and strive to do it to the best of your ability. Your self-discipline is unwavering and you cannot be distracted until the task is completed. You are capable of doing work that demands a high degree of precision and perfection, work that others may shun due to its monotonous nature. While material things preoccupy you, you are not attracted to the spiritual realm.

You are able to converse about automobiles for hours, but an evening of poetry scares you off. Your schedule is so organized that it is difficult to make changes in your daily routine. You run your life meticulously and require order at home and in your head.

However, you are narrow-minded and not open to things and ideas that are new and different than those you already know.

If you were to broaden your horizons and allow yourself to open up to new worlds, you would find enjoyment in many things that you never even dreamed of doing or trying. Opening yourself up to new ideas and breaking away from rigidity would only be to your benefit.

5. The numerological analysis of number 4 according to consonants

You have an neat appearance and enjoy organization and order. You are very pragmatic and meticulously adhere to an organized schedule. (It seems that in this case, a description that is brief and to the point is most suited to Number 4.)

6. The numerological analysis of number 4 according to the date of birth

Tremendous effort is necessary in order to attain the hoped-for results. Focus on the details and work thoroughly without compromising. Equip yourself with great spiritual strength and take a deep breath in preparation for the long haul ahead. Life requires that you practice self-control and restrain your impulses.

It is advisable to focus on the spiritual and the inner self, and not on external behavior and etiquette. Inner contemplation is necessary and is the right thing for you. At times, your emotional life ends up in failure and disappointment. Strong, stable mental foundations temper negative feelings. You are able to compromise and exercise moderation.

Extreme behavior will not lead to any development whatsoever, and therefore it is worthwhile to avoid rigidity and let your thoughts flow in various directions. Let your intuition lead you and make you attentive to what your heart has to say. Positive development will occur if you choose the path of compromise and openness to other opinions, new ideas, and original ways of thinking.

Avoid blaming others, especially when there is no solid evidence for doing so. People are never certain about the course that life may take, and are therefore in a constant state of apprehension and worry.

You are able to carry a burden and suffer without complaining or revealing how difficult it is.

Your ability to exercise restraint will stand you in good stead throughout your life.

7. The numerological analysis of number 4 according to the birthday

You find it difficult to cope with change. Try to anticipate change and plan for it emotionally. There may be surprises in your family life, but they are less threatening.

This is a period of renewal. You have a strong desire to face your past mistakes and turn over a new leaf. Take advantage of the openness that characterizes this period of life to learn the lessons of the past. Be brave enough to implement them.

By nature, you enjoy routine. Therefore, it is advisable that you do everything in your power to weather these temporary disturbances quietly and return to a routine that brings you peace of mind and plenty of self-confidence. Pay careful attention to family-related problems, and mobilize all your efforts in order to solve them in the easiest way possible, without causing unnecessary commotion.

8. The numerological analysis of number 4 according to the nine-year cycle

A year of financial progress. The reason for this might be a promotion at work or the start of a new business. You must be practical and responsible. Plan your steps in advance; be thoughtful and decisive. You should not leave things to fate or be hasty. It is advisable not to work too hard; do not overdo things.

You should not act based on your discretion alone, even if your intuition is usually correct. In this case, it is preferable not to act spontaneously or rely on your senses, but to rely on cold logic alone. Do not let external diversions distract you from your goals. You have to show determination in order to succeed. Try to eliminate distractions and concentrate on the task at hand.

Try to be more assertive as this year offers opportunities for progress and success. Consequently, those who come in contact with you will respect you and hold you in high esteem.

Do not underestimate yourself. You radiate self-confidence. The more you develop your sense of self-respect and believe in your abilities and endeavors, the better those in your environment will relate to you. Control yourself and do not let yourself get dragged under by the ceaseless undertow of ambition. Devote time to your home and family.

9. The numerological analysis of number 4 according to the

partnership number

The partners must reach completeness in their life together. They must learn to implement ideas, initiate and organize. This is the catalyst for their life together. The better they are at working together toward joint objectives, the stronger their ties will be. Idleness and inertia may dull their life.

Even if they are not blessed with a high energy level, it is worthwhile to be busy: producing, planning, organizing, initiating, being in action. Creative thinking produces new ideas. If the partners are idle, they will very soon experience boredom and tedium that will undermine their relationship.

10. The numerological analysis of number 4 in raising children

The number 4 child requires stability. In times of need, he depends on the family unit and those closest to him for support. By providing him with warmth and love, the family serves as the most significant framework in his life. He is a "mama's boy." He likes to hide behind his mother's skirts and be as close to her as possible. His parents must try to give him a sense of stability that will help him deal with the difficulties he is bound to face in day-to-day life. The child must learn to adapt himself to the harsh surroundings in which we live. He must know that life is not always easy and that, at times, it is difficult to cope. He must learn to get along on his own. He must understand that Mom and Dad cannot be with him 24 hours a day, and that he will often have to make his own way in life. If he internalizes these principles and acquires a basic degree of confidence, he will be able to go out into the world and take upon himself tasks and decisions.

The number 4 child is sensitive and full of compassion for every living being. He loves animals, and if it were up to him, the house would be full of abandoned creatures found in the street. He enjoys helping out and always volunteers for any task.

His highly developed imagination and sensitivity make him easily anxious and frightened. The parents must pay attention to his fears and help him overcome them. He should be encouraged to talk about his anxieties and express his fears concerning the outside world. Uncompromising support and an understanding of his difficulties are likely to help him to overcome these anxieties and fears.

11. The numerological analysis of number 4 according to the first and

last name

You are organized and methodical. You know that only through hard, intensive work will you achieve maximum results. Work requiring precision and attention to detail suits you.

You are very disciplined, and when you set objectives for yourself, you achieve them at all costs. You are willing to forego other things as long as the fruits of your labor are perfect, at minimum cost and with maximum investment. You are gifted with a highly developed sense of responsibility and therefore others tend to trust you. You are honest and straightforward. These qualities help you in your professional life, but at times, within the jungle of modern society, you are perceived as naive.

Occasionally, you find yourself utilizing obsolete methods because of your fear of technology. You must be more open to new ideas. If you do so, you will be more efficient, and it will prove helpful both to yourself and to your surroundings. You are a perfectionist. You do not compromise on less than the best. You are bound by rigid conventions and expect others to be like you. You must be more aware of this tendency, since people are inclined to interpret such behavior as cruel and hard-hearted.

You tend to take things to heart. This might affect your health adversely, so you should make sure to take breaks from your fast-paced lifestyle – by taking a vacation, for example. It would be good if you had a regular program of physical fitness and watched your diet.

Always try to see the half-full rather than half-empty glass. This will teach you to enjoy the fruits of your efforts. You must be happy and smile more often.

12. The numerological analysis of number 4 according to cosmic vibrations

The number 4 represents the formation of matter, that is, the creation of volume. The creation of this number gave corporeality to reality. The number 4 contributed the third dimension (height) to the universe, and from now on, length, breadth, and height exist.

The number 4 gave rise to the fourth point, and now it was possible to create a primal shape with volume, such as a three-sided pyramid. This pyramid has properties of length, breadth, and height, and rests on a base comprising three points (three angles). A fourth point, which is located above them, forms the apex of the pyramid.

The number 4 is represented and symbolized by means of a square: ❏

Number 5

1. The numerological analysis of number 5 according to the traditional approach known as "the numerology of Agricola"

Number 5 people are clever, joyful, resourceful and adventurous at heart. They enjoy visiting new places and being exposed to new ideas. Diligent, alert, and impeccably tasteful, they sometimes tend to be overly critical, especially toward themselves.

They are individualistic and selective, and love reading and researching. They are very bright and will never waste their time on dead-end pursuits. They are good organizers and can successfully get others to perform unpleasant or boring tasks. They are original and creative people.

In spite of their success, many constantly fear failure. Number 5 people generally excel in the arts, medicine, commerce, archeology, and teaching. They can succeed in so many areas that their real problem revolves around choosing their field of specialization. They are attracted to everything, but nothing "grabs" them.

They are multifaceted – as reflected in the shape of the pentagon. They are likely to be unpredictable, inconsiderate and uncompromising toward themselves. Generally speaking, they are attractive, gregarious and truly empathetic. They recover quickly from life's blows. Many of them are troubled by anxieties, though externally they are able to maintain a serene facade.

In love, they are faithful, overflowing with warmth and generosity, and become jealous and suspicious only if given good grounds. They do not like to argue, but if dragged into a conflict, they will stand up for themselves.

They are very helpful to those close to them, offering generous financial aid, and are always willing to give any type of practical assistance needed.

Usually, number 5 people do not like to ask others for help. They enjoy comfort, hate waste, and are willing to have good relationships with relatives as long as the latter do not interfere with their lives.

The number 5 represents nature and the senses. It is sometimes considered to mean marriage, but generally, it symbolizes the body – human physicality. Five is known to alchemists as "essence" since it is a combination of four elements which constitute a fifth quality: material life and physical consciousness.

Five represents human beings: They have two arms, two legs, and a head, and therefore may be seen as a five-pointed star.

The Romans believed that a pentagonal-shaped talisman would protect them from witches and evil spirits.

2. The numerological analysis of number 5 according to characteristics of love and sexuality

When it comes to love and sexuality, number 5 people are in the middle: They exhibit all the positive characteristics concerning love and sex, as well as all the negative ones. Consequently, their approach is nervous, jumpy and unpredictable.

Number 5 people's sexuality is not remarkably good, but their enthusiasm and single-mindedness make up for it. Many say that they have a magnet inside them, that is, they are influenced by and attracted to external factors in their environment. These factors are attracted to them, too. And then, when the objective of their attentions changes, the magnet changes its course.

Number 5 people are the type of lovers written about in books. They are the jealous and unfaithful lovers who appear in criminal reports in the media. They are the ones people follow blindly... or recoil from!

The central issue concerning number 5 people is the ability to allow a sexual and love relationship to develop beyond a one-night stand. And this is a real problem. Their lives are full of crises, and ups and downs when it comes to this important realm.

Number 5 people are quite a gamble for numerology. They are unpredictable, and numerologists find it difficult to characterize them in view of their nature. But it is important to remember that love and sex are actually the triggers – the prime movers – of emotional life for these people.

3. The numerological analysis of number 5 according to astro-numerology

This refers to those born on the fifth, fourteenth or twenty-third days of the month.

Mercury is the factor on the birth chart that enables us to understand and take advantage of the nature of the universe, the natural world and human nature itself – while we adapt and change.

Mercury grants us the opportunity to understand and adapt various systems to our needs, for example, the musical scale (including speech); the nature of color... and numerology!

Mercury is influential in the field of communications, but this is not its original expression. At its source, Mercury is the factor allowing us to take advantage of opportunities, and only with its aid can we ascend from one stage to the next.

It may be said that even when opportunities are spread out around us, only Mercury will allow us to exploit them, soaring sky-high with them.

Number 5 is similar in essence to Mercury. Even when it is the individual's personal number, it tells us: "Take advantage of the opportunities presented to you!"

Number 5 is a number that demands a high degree of equilibrium, otherwise it will cause the person to express himself incorrectly.

It may be claimed – in general, of course – that a person with number 5 who is not balanced by a number 2 or 7 may find himself involved in deviant behavior.

Number 5, like Mercury, is the channel through which a person connects with his environment, not only in the sense of communication, but also in the sense of the reciprocity between him and his surroundings.

4. The numerological analysis of number 5 according to vowels

You are impulsive. It is difficult for you to control your momentary impulses, and you often find that they take control of you and divert you from your original intentions.

You enjoy change to the point of obsession. If a week goes by without some special thrill, you will devise something to get excited about. You cannot remain calm for even a minute.

You must always be in motion, and if you are not able to give vent to your impulses, you feel as if you are imprisoned. You like taking risks and walking on the fine line between a sane and orderly life and a crazy one full of experiences. Given your addictive personality, gambling, alcohol and so forth are tempting. You are advised to stick to the tasks at hand and control your dangerous urges.

You are sexy. Easily attracted to the opposite sex, you allow your fantasies to lead you down dubious paths that others would not even dare to imagine.

You are obviously not one for routine work. If you were able to get away with not working at all and spend your days enjoying yourself, you would be in seventh heaven.

All this aside, you must develop a sense of responsibility and always be involved in the type of work that offers thrills and changes. If you choose a monotonous and routine job, you will not hold on to it for long. If you do indeed aspire to succeed in life and achieve high status at work or in business, you must learn to control your impulsive nature and focus on your objective.

5. The numerological analysis of number 5 according to consonants

You are an interesting and unusual person, one who is considered unique and different by others. Gifted with a highly developed verbal skill, you keep your audience riveted with no difficulty. You are a multifaceted person, knowledgeable in a wide variety of fields. It appears that you are never bored. You will always find some interest in whatever you are doing, and invariably persist in your desire to investigate and delve into the deeper essence of things.

You abhor superficiality and shallow people. You radiate a love of life and adventure, enjoying special, unusual, and different things. Occasionally, you are willing to take risks or act spontaneously for the fun of it or just to be unique and different.

It is important for you to give free rein to your uniqueness. You love receiving compliments and have no problem complimenting others. You do not find it difficult to say something nice or put in a good word for a friend. You are honest, and hypocrisy is beyond you.

Although esthetics are important to you, first and foremost your friends must be smart and sensible; their external appearance is secondary in your eyes. However, you yourself always see to it that you look your best. At the same time, you deem it important to display your intellectual prowess.

Members of the opposite sex are attracted to you. You become bored quickly in a serious relationship and prefer changing partners frequently. Sex is central to your life, and it is rare that you find yourself without a partner for any length of time.

6. The numerological analysis of number 5 according to the date of birth

The direction of your life indicates surprises, changes and new experiences. You have the desire to examine, know, and try out as much as possible. Your impulses drive you toward special and interesting fields. You will not rest until you have delved deeply into the essence of things – investigating, comparing and studying their secrets. It is important for you to learn and develop, and you often do this at the expense of other important undertakings. As the wise King Solomon said, "Life and death are in the hands of the tongue." Be alert to nuances and subtleties; emphasize that which must be expressed and downplay that which is destructive. If you choose to take advantage of the endless possibilities available to you, first take time to think and plan carefully, rather than acting on impulse. In your case, freedom of action parallels freedom of thought. Learn to control your desires and wishes, and try not to be swept away by emotion and urges of the moment. You have a strong desire to follow your momentary desires and attain immediate gratification. Do not give in to them. Grappling with them may lead to clarity of mind and the possibility of controlling them. However, pay careful attention to these desires and be aware of their physical manifestations and what are saying. Relationships with members of the opposite sex are important and will help you get to know your inner self. Facing new situations and people of the opposite sex gives rise to feelings that are sometimes not expressed and creates opportunities to undergo new and interesting experiences. Do not reject these opportunities, even if they sometimes appear too risky at first.

7. The numerological analysis of number 5 according to the birthday

The focus here is on business. This period provides opportunities for becoming financially established. You focus and concentrate on what you do, without giving in or compromising when it comes to quality. The actions you take during this period will serve as milestones for your future, both in life in general and in business in particular.

You are open to meeting new people and your communication with your surroundings will blossom in the near future. The long-term effects will be revealed through your growing trust of others.

During this time of life, your managerial abilities may emerge. Even if you never thought yourself capable of such work, this is a good chance to move into positions of management and supervision. Those hidden aspirations might now be realized. Be courageous and implement your ideas.

8. The numerological analysis of number 5 according to the nine-year cycle

This is a year that brings variety to your life, and you should be rational and calm as it goes by. It is a year in which you will learn to recognize the differences between people.

You will learn to appreciate opinions and ideas that oppose your own, and to hear them out with patience and understanding. During this year, you will find out whether you are a sociable person or not – one who is easily assimilated into society, likes other people and is open, or one who is more reserved and tends not to form immediate ties with others.

It is a good year to become involved in things that seemed a waste of time in previous years. During this period, you will learn to appreciate the importance of taking up leisure activities and to value the new content that they bring to your life, as well as the unique character and energies that they provide in an otherwise routine existence. A new relationship will infuse your life with "new blood" and make you feel young again.

9. The numerological analysis of number 5 according to the

partnership number

This number indicates the need to learn to accept the concept of a process, of things changing. An unrestrained life together – in which the partners are unable to maintain a balance, to plan ahead or to be rational, but rather usually behave as if they have been swept along by their feelings or actions – is liable to end badly.

The more the partners control their passions and immediate needs as well as delay gratification, the more planned and organized their life will be. This is likely to bring order into their lives, and this order will give them a sense of greater self-confidence, leading to the right way of life.

10. The numerological analysis of number 5 in raising children

The number 5 child's need for activity must be channeled in positive directions. He must be encouraged to get involved in sports. He has the ability to succeed in this field and it is therefore a good one to adopt. At the same time, he is also enchanted by stories and the arts. He can become totally engrossed in a riveting story. He has such a high level of concentration that he may detach himself completely from his surroundings. All branches of the arts interest him, but it is particularly worthwhile to focus on crafts such as carpentry, model-building (such as miniature airplanes), and other activities that require precision and patience. He needs to express himself and his talents, and is very active. He finds it easy to concentrate on a particular activity – but only if it fascinates him. If something interests him, he is able to keep at it for a lengthy period of time. If not, he will fritter the time away without any serious objective.

The child's concentration must be developed so that he will make the best use of his spare time. He requires both guidance and parents who are prepared to make an effort to give him the tools he needs. If he is not given a direction, he will go off the rails. He does not have the ability to occupy himself and take an interest in something without external stimulation. It would be a shame if his talents were wasted and not properly exploited.

11. The numerological analysis of number 5 according to the first and

last name

You are bubbly and love life – and quite unable to enjoy a quiet, tranquil lifestyle. You always need new stimuli and interesting challenges to keep you going.

You should try to be more patient and understanding. It is not easy for your partner to keep up with your frantic pace. Changes – which you are not only used to, but even require – may be threatening to your partner and may alienate him/her. Take life easier and more calmly.

You should choose a profession that involves working with people.

Make an effort to be calmer and more tranquil, less volatile and impulsive, and try not to become quickly addicted to various passions, as you are liable to do.

You must strive for a more balanced, full and whole life. This will make it easier for you to cope with your surroundings.

12. The numerological analysis of number 5 according to cosmic vibrations

The number 5 represents the formation of primeval life on earth by means of the spirit of God (which is represented by the number 1), which came down to reside in matter (which is represented by the number 4). In other words, the spirit of God was embodied in flesh and blew the breath of life into it. This is the origin of the belief that the number 5 represents man and not animals, which do not contain the spirit of the Creator.

Number 5 is represented by a five-pointed star.

Number 6

1. The numerological analysis of number 6 according to the traditional

approach known as "the numerology of Agricola"

Number 6 people are creative, resourceful, trusting and trustworthy. They are idealists who love beauty, have a developed imagination, and are happiest when engaged in creative activities. They possess an excellent sense of color and many are outstandingly skilled in one of the arts. They are generally successful and are capable of becoming rich and powerful. Among them, there are many highly gifted artists, sculptors, writers, musicians, and teachers.

Numerologists claim that those whose number is 6 are highly successful in the arts due to the fact that 6 is two times 3 (3+3 = 6), and 3 is an "honorable" number.

They are blessed with moral courage, a sensitive heart, and the skill to conduct negotiations. They intuitively understand the needs and difficulties of others, and are able to bring out their best.

Six is the only number of the nine discussed which can be divided both by an even number (2) as well as by an odd number (3).

Number 6 people are balanced, open and self-controlled. They can be good debaters, since they are able to understand both sides of an argument without prejudice. They possess unique charm, and are often physically attractive and dignified. They can be stubborn, arrogant, and forgiving toward themselves.

In love, they overflow with warmth and are faithful partners. They tend to worry about their partner's loyalty, but are able to hide these feelings as long as they are secure in the relationship. If their sense of dignity and decency is severely offended, they will not hesitate to terminate the relationship forthwith. After marriage, they usually prefer the company of their spouse, but keep in touch with good friends.

They enjoy comfortable and orderly homes and are home bodies, though not to the extreme. They will always be fair and considerate, loathe arguments and are willing to do anything to prevent them, although they can be sharp-tongued and sarcastic if they are dragged into a quarrel. They are very generous toward friends and loved ones who need their help. They are empathetic and willing to help perform boring or unpleasant tasks, if necessary.

Number 6 people never ask for help, relying on themselves alone. They despise receiving favors, and many are troubled by the fear of dependence in old age. They are not especially interested in money as long as no financial difficulties arise. Nevertheless, they have an aversion to waste and are generally thrifty. They are devoted parents and keep up a long-term and loving relationship with their children.

2. The numerological analysis of number 6 according to characteristics of love and sexuality

It is common knowledge that number 6 people are under the influence of the planet Venus. Consequently, most numerologists conclude that love, ruled by Venus, is the primary energy nurturing these individuals. (Some numerologists go as far as saying that number 6 people must always find number 9 partners, who are ruled by the energy of Mars. In this way, a perfect match is achieved: 6+9.)

Modern numerology attempts to examine the personal number without reference to the planets. But in order to reach profound and thorough interpretations, together with suggestions for action, numerologists examine number 6 through the Star of David (six-pointed star).

The shape of the Star of David is two superimposed triangles, one pointing upward, and the other downward. Numerologists view the first triangle as the triangle of sexuality, and the second as the triangle of love. The first and fundamental problem of these individuals is to preserve the balance of the two triangles. If not, the Star of David will disintegrate into separate, meaningless components.

Therefore, number 6 people work at balancing love and sexuality, dedicating their entire lives to this task, both with regard to themselves and their spouses. This is not an easy chore, as this balance comes naturally to few people and demands a considerable and long-term effort.

Practically speaking, number 6 people seek a balance between love and sexuality, and we cannot predict to what degree these two factors will actually balance each other.

Number 6 people do not concern themselves with the question of degree, but rather concentrate on seeking balance.

3. The numerological analysis of number 6 according to astro-numerology

This refers to those born on the sixth, fifteenth or twenty-fourth days of the month.

Number 6, like Venus, is an essential factor in a person's life. The symbol for Venus is known as the symbol of female sexuality, but its essence is much stronger than that. It symbolizes the union between the masculine forces, the elements of air and fire, and the feminine forces, the elements of earth and water. (The four are symbolized by the cross.) The circle in the symbol represents eternal union, a union which is the basis of the cyclical nature of the universe.

Venus is an ancient symbol. In ancient Egypt, it was always held in the hands of the royal couple, whose role it was to perpetuate the Pharaoh's dynasty. Following its role in Egypt, Venus became the symbol of sexuality in general. Later, when Mars came to be considered the masculine principle, and sexuality was separated from the ability to conceive and give birth, Venus was mainly recognized as a feminine sexual symbol.

Venus is connected to beauty, but not only physical beauty; rather, it is beauty that is both spiritual and creative. In fact, it speaks to the concept of true love or pure beauty.

Venus in an unfavorable position is always a "trap" – passionate impulses not finding a positive direction. A well-located Venus on the chart always indicates the immense power love has in one's life.

Number 6 moves us one step ahead. It determines how balance in life, equilibrium, is obtained by the ability to love.

Number 6 is not one of the numbers that must appear on a numerological chart. However, if it is missing, it testifies to a lack of balance in one's life.

4. The numerological analysis of number 6 according to vowels

You are a classic family-oriented person. You prefer to neglect your career and anything else that may threaten your family and happiness – since for you happiness is linked to the amount of time spent with your family. You enjoy art and poetry.

The appearance of your home is very important to you, as you feel that it mirrors your inner self. The interior design influences your personality directly. You devote a great deal of attention to detail. You are blessed with a sense of responsibility and a desire to envelop those around you in infinite love. You must be aware of the fact that, at times, you are too generous with your love, and you should set some limits in this regard. Allow those around you, particularly family members, freedom. They are so important to you that your concern for their welfare is liable to drive you mad.

Calm down. Try to be less obsessive in your sense of responsibility towards your family. The more space you allow yourself and others, the more comfortable you will feel. You would also receive more positive feedback. Be open and broaden your horizons. Your natural characteristics and talents would manifest themselves to a greater extent if you focused on your abilities. Try to control your urge to constantly know what each member of your family is doing; you would waste less energy worrying. They will do just as well (if not better) without you pressuring them, whether consciously or subconsciously.

5. The numerological analysis of number 6 according to consonants

You are a warm person who likes to shower others with love. You enjoy the warmth of the family unit. The members of your family constitute the most important element in your life – first and foremost, your children. You are generally crazy about children, and love your own to distraction. If your domestic life is successful, you will always be happy, since you believe that the pinnacle of happiness and success lies in a good family life.

Despite the fact that you are very devoted and faithful – at work too – you are the type of parent who will get home as early as possible in order to spend time with the children, bathe them, and put them to bed.

You like helping others and have a highly developed sense of responsibility. When you are in the vicinity, your friends know there is someone on whom they can depend. Nevertheless, you have a strong character and are assertive to the extent that no one will dare make a sucker out of you or take advantage of your good nature.

You are very sober and view reality objectively. You are not a wimp and know how to stand up for yourself and be tough when necessary. You also know how to cope with the difficulties of day-to-day living and face the rougher sides of life.

Since you enjoy looking good, neat and rather elegant, you are fussy about your appearance. Physical activity is important and you make sure to set aside time for it during the week. You are gifted with a special sensitivity for *objets d'art*, and usually enjoy decorating your home with expensive and valuable pieces.

6. The numerological analysis of number 6 according to the date of birth

This indicates responsibility. Helping others is your top priority. Learn to control situations. Each action you take during your life should be taken in the spirit of love, and the desire to give and share. Your ability to empathize and identify with others is beneficial and serves your objectives. It presents endless possibilities to undertake a task and implement it. Your ability to face the future fearlessly gives you renewed strengths.

Given your excellent language and verbal skills, you are a good negotiator and a great orator. Your desire to help and be a good listener to those in trouble is a result of your ability to love. You are motivated by ambition and a desire to achieve. You never rest until the entire task is completed to the very last detail. You have broad vision and are able to cooperate with those around you. As a result of your sincere desire to cooperate and help, you succeed.

7. The numerological analysis of number 6 according to the birthday

This is a good time to take a break from work and do things around the house. If your home is in need of renovations or repairs, this is the right time to do them. It is not a good time for travel or for leaving the home and family. This is the time, more than ever, that it is vital to listen to family members, offer them help when needed, and stay close by!

It is also an excellent time to bring the family together; you should take advantage of it, since it will influence later periods of life and help ensure open and honest relationships with family members. Decisions should be made after due consideration and planning. All possible risks should be recognized and taken into account.

During this period, you may experience confusion and dissatisfaction, and it is therefore advisable to act thoughtfully and responsibly, *not* allowing things to take their own course.

8. *The numerological analysis of number 6 according to the nine-year cycle*

This year provides elements of stability regarding all the basic components of life: home, family, work, and friends. This is a year during which you can make changes and decisions that will turn out for the best.

It is an excellent year for developing creativity. Get involved in the various aspects of the arts, handiwork, and crafts.

The year will provide a good and positive atmosphere for study, and will inspire confidence, self-discipline and self-control. Involvement in the arts and spiritual things could become so significant that the general course of your life may change.

It is crucial not to dominate those around you, not to discriminate against others, not to brand people with stigmas and not to employ a double standard.

And finally, this is a year in which you will learn to appreciate pure, honest love, without the need to receive anything in exchange or "settle accounts" with the other side.

9. *The numerological analysis of number 6 according to the*

partnership number

The partners must learn to take responsibility and not blame each other every time something happens. Developing creativity is crucial for living together. Giving free rein to positive energies and using creativity to express what is deep in the soul is most welcome. The partners must learn to love!

The ability to open their hearts to love generally and unconditionally will provide the partners with a new perspective on their relationship.

10. *The numerological analysis of number 6 in raising children*

The number 6 child has a special sensitivity for beauty and harmony. He enjoys giving and receiving love, is sensitive to the beauty of the world and knows how to appreciate the loveliness of a flower or sense the joy of falling raindrops. He is excited by nature and knows how to express himself and involve others around him. His sensitivity to nature makes him an unusual child whose friends may not always understand what he is carrying on about. He is enthusiastic about things that other children tend to be indifferent to or take for granted. He is full of *joie de vivre*, and is temperamental and creative. He has artistic talents that he manifests by means of various projects, just like a little artist. He asks about anything he does not understand and wants to delve deeply into various phenomena and subjects. At times, it can prove tiring to his parents, who find it difficult to satisfy his curiosity. However, they should be pleased that he is inquisitive and knowledgeable, as this sets him apart from other children.

This type of child must be given a chance to express himself without being told what to do or how to think. His fertile imagination should be allowed to lead him and develop his ability for free and independent thought.

11. The numerological analysis of number 6 according to the first and

last name

You have the ability to give generously of yourself to those around you, without limitations. You are endowed with a highly developed sense of morality and justice, and social injustice enrages and revolts you.

You are able to put yourself in other people's shoes. The caring professions, such as social work or teaching, suit you. You are very generous and willing to share whatever you have with others, even if you have very little.

Your appearance is important to you. You are attracted to partners whose outstanding qualities are gentleness and fragility, and you eschew the company of vulgar people. You believe in working hard in order to achieve your objectives. You cannot stand receiving personal benefits or taking advantage of connections, and will always choose the longer but safer path over risky shortcuts.

Family is of utmost importance and you try to help out at home as much as possible. Your loved ones are so important to you that you sometimes clip their wings and do not allow them the freedom to do their own thing.

Do not rush to reveal your emotions in a new relationship. Occasionally, you are carried away by feelings and may end up disappointed. You must learn to navigate more independently through life and rely on yourself alone. Do not let others take advantage of your good-heartedness or your tendency to give of yourself limitlessly. Learn to give in moderation, otherwise you will find that others take advantage of you, possibly causing irreparable harm.

12. The numerological analysis of number 6 according to cosmic vibrations

The number 6 represents harmony. This number restored to the universe the equilibrium that had been upset by the number 5.

The number 6 represents a philosophy of life that can observe reality from different points of view.

The number 6 is represented and symbolized by a Star of David.

This shape comprises two superimposed triangles that symbolize the balance between opposites.

Number 7

1. The numerological analysis of number 7 according to the traditional

approach known as "the numerology of Agricola"

Number 7 people are diligent and creative, and tend to be involved in mysticism and the occult. They often have ESP. They are unique and brilliant, and occasionally need to withdraw from society in order to center themselves. They have a strong spirit and are gifted with the ability to penetrate the unknown, link the practical to the theoretical and the conventional to the unconventional. They enjoy travel, and actively seek truths relating to the nature and meaning of the universe beyond superficial approaches, which by no means satisfy them.

Number 7 people, however, are likely to be pessimistic, sarcastic, and indifferent, and tend to isolate themselves. They are threatened by danger – their imagination and intuition can get the better of their rational mind to the extent that they can lose control and orientation, and drift away into fantasy and dreams.

Generally speaking, they consider neither money nor material comforts to be important. However, they should take care not to neglect their material needs, since it is easier to develop in a peaceful and protected environment.

They are reserved, impressive, and artistic individuals, and often succeed as scientists, inventors, psychiatrists, writers, musicians, painters, and sculptors.

When it comes to love, they are sensitive, ardent, and understanding, while not particularly jealous. Nevertheless, if angered, they are liable to end a relationship icily. They are good-tempered and pleasant; though they detest arguments, they insist on immediately resolving disagreements by means of frank discussion in an attempt to reach a satisfactory solution. After marriage, they become more interested in their careers and success, not necessarily to support a life of luxury, but rather to provide their loved ones with a fine and comfortable home. Usually, they do not have the faintest idea about financial planning and calculations, leaving these to their spouse. They are able to treat their relatives with a certain degree of affection, but do not really show an interest in them.

The symbol of number 7 is a triangle constructed on a square, a shape that represents cyclical time in the cosmos and in human life. Dr. Wayne Westcott discovered a connection between the number 7 and the development of the human infant: After seven days the umbilical cord drops off; after two weeks (twice seven) the eyes begin to see; after three weeks (three times seven) the baby begins to turn his head; after seven months his teeth start to grow; after fourteen months (twice seven) he is able to sit steadily; and after twenty-eight months (four times seven) he can walk confidently.

The number 7 is considered a particularly lucky and important number. According to ancient traditions, 7 symbolizes the victory of spirit over matter. Joshua circled the walls of Jericho for seven days until they fell.

In the Book of Revelations in the New Testament, the number 7 appears frequently: seven churches, seven golden candlesticks, seven stars, seven lamps of fire, seven seals and seven kings. Tradition claims that the seventh son of a seventh son is gifted with magical powers. There are seven days in a week, seven colors in the spectrum, and the phases of the moon change visibly every seven days.

2. The numerological analysis of number 7 according to characteristics of love and sexuality

Number 7 people are particularly vulnerable to the energies of love and sex. This means that these individuals want to be "in love", to "fulfill" their sexuality, and to "radiate" love. In other words, the impression is just as important as the actual fact.

Naturally, number 7 people expose this aspect of their lives in times of a separation or break-up.

Have you ever been present in the love nest of a number 7 who is worn out?! He acts as if he has been stripped and paraded through the town square with all of his acquaintances throwing rotten eggs at him!

For this reason, their sensitivity, not to mention their vulnerability, is especially evident during times of crisis, or when they are "between relationships." As a result, they live on the edge when it comes to their love lives and sexuality, expending a lot of energy and exertion in this area of life.

This is the reason that many of these individuals prefer "theory" to "practice", in other words, they choose the spiritual side of love rather than its material, physical side.

3. The numerological analysis of number 7 according to astro-numerology

This refers to those born on the seventh, sixteenth or twenty-fifth days of the month. *(And uniquely in this case, people whose number is 7 as a result of a numerological combination of their first and mother's names, also exhibit qualities related to the astro-numerological analysis of number 7.)*

Neptune influences the individual on a slightly different plane, a higher plane than we have discussed until now. It might be said that Neptune (Poseidon), ruler of the seas, the god of Atlantis, sought a new stratum in the material world. This stratum, or plane, is inner awareness.

In the astrological chart, Neptune serves as a higher version of Venus – love that is not dependent upon anything else – as well as a balancing force to Mercury. In the birth chart, Neptune gives a person the ability to penetrate deeply into his consciousness, and Neptune in an unfavorable position threatens what would be considered a healthy approach to the opposing worlds of reality and spirit.

However, in numerology, number 7 is much more significant. The number's mystic and magical importance cannot be ignored: 7 days in the week, 7 primary planets, 7 heavens, 7 chakras, etc. The number 7 opens the door to the person's higher consciousness, and to that of humanity.

It should be understood that as the planets get further away from the earth – and Neptune is a "distant" planet – their astrological influence on human beings diminishes. However, their numerological influence increases!

4. The numerological analysis of number 7 according to vowels

Your character is that of a mystic. You pursue knowledge and seek a connection with your higher self – the soul. This trait may alienate you from others whose orientation is more earthy. Do not let yourself get carried away. Although this is very difficult, try to plant both feet on the ground. The more you succeed, the better your connection with your environment will be. People will understand you and you will find it easy to forge connections and make friends. The more you close yourself off in the bubble that transports you to mystical realms, the more difficult it will be for you to function socially. However, it is your choice alone.

You aspire to acquire knowledge and are not lenient with yourself in the process. When you want to achieve an objective, almost nothing stands in your way. You seek perfection in everyday situations as well as in more significant and serious endeavors. Beware of your natural tendency to be over-engrossed in spirituality. It might become an obstacle in your path to perfection.

5. The numerological analysis of number 7 according to consonants

You are shy and enjoy being alone. As an individualist, it is not always easy for you to communicate with others, particularly if they are strangers. You do not like sharing your experiences with others, even if they are very close to you.

You always look good, taking care to appear and dress well; you dislike looking unkempt.

You do not like being conspicuous and are always shy and retiring. Quiet by nature, you enjoy calm and tranquillity rather than public events or noisy parties. You invariably prefer quiet, peaceful entertainment such as a movie or a meal in a fine restaurant to an evening at a nightclub.

You enjoy being involved in spiritual things and aspire to achieve wholeness and nirvana. You tend to float in higher worlds; do not forget, however, that what keeps you afloat is equilibrium. You must therefore pay attention to the fine line between a healthy interest in the inner self and the soul – which provides you with equilibrium – and an extreme preoccupation with them that will upset it.

You must learn to be more down-to-earth. Strive to be more sober and not get carried away into spiritual realms that take you too far from those around you, causing you to lose the everyday connection with them. Take care not to get addicted to spiritualism and mysticism. There are people around you who love you, and those relationships are too important for you to jeopardize them.

6. The numerological analysis of number 7 according to the date of birth

Your perspective on life is unique. Look beyond the physical world to the path you must take. Spirituality constitutes an integral part of your life. You must aspire to a spiritual life as much as possible, and spend time on inner contemplation pertaining to the soul and God.

Strive to excel and specialize in a specific field. You must be very strong on the emotional level and know how to take criticism. It is important for you to be connected to your environment, feel the true rhythm of life around you and react as an integral part of society.

7. The numerological analysis of number 7 according to the birthday

Your spiritual nature will come to the fore and therefore you should be open to change and allow energies to flow freely. Your inner power is growing, and with it, your capacity to cope in times of crisis. You will emerge stronger from this period. Your self-confidence will increase and you will be more aware of the emotional processes taking place in your life.

Be aware of any physical change or any problem. The more you are aware of your body, the easier it will be to overcome health problems and catch them at an early stage. Do not neglect your health. Your body is exposed to crises at the moment, which may affect your constitution. Prepare yourself for this.

Money that you have been expecting will be delayed. Proper money management is crucial at this time. Do not make mistakes and assess your business correctly. Only in this way will you ensure your economic status and security.

8. The numerological analysis of number 7 according to the nine-year cycle

This is a good year for the spirit – a year of spirituality. However, do not flee from reality; make sure you have both feet firmly planted on the ground.

Concentrate on the present and on the future. Dwelling on past mistakes will not be helpful to your progress; on the contrary, it will cause you to remain in the same place. Instead of concentrating on the past, try new modes of action and move forward.

The more you introspect, the easier it will be for you to examine your inherent abilities. During this year, you will be able to arrive at your inner truth. It is a good time for soul-searching.

You are standing at a crossroads in life, trying to decide which path to follow in the coming years. Giving to others and doing things for their welfare may contribute significantly to the feeling of wholeness you yearn for.

9. The numerological analysis of number 7 according to the

partnership number

The partners must work together spiritually and develop their intuitive abilities. Sensitivity – going into detail and developing the rare skill of discerning subtleties – is likely to improve interpersonal relations substantially. If both partners "broadcast" emotions and thoughts and "sense" each other, they can expect to live together in harmony.

10. The numerological analysis of number 7 in raising children

The number 7 child must learn to be open and attentive to others. He has a tendency to escape from reality into imaginary worlds. Relationships with others will force him to return to reality and face situations in which he will have to show determination and stand up for his rights. The parents' role is to provide him with the knowledge he will require to make his way through the complexities of life. He is able to give of himself limitlessly. He must be guided and made to understand the importance of setting limits in his relationships with others. He is not assertive. If he acquires the correct ways and behavior patterns, they will be useful to him throughout his life. His parents would do well to set him on a clear and correct path. Guidelines and directions – if given in the correct amount and at the appropriate time – will help him learn about the world he lives in. On the other hand, unnecessary interference, exaggerated demands and aggressive intrusion into his personal space will achieve the opposite results and undermine his self-confidence.

11. The numerological analysis of number 7 according to the first and

last name

Since you have been blessed with special spiritual qualities, you are able to help others as well as yourself. However, you will have to practice using this trait, as it does not manifest itself automatically. You possess sensitivities that others do not. You do not need other people to make you experience wholeness or enjoyment, as you are able to provide yourself with everything you need – interests, curiosity and a quest for knowledge.

Your natural spiritual qualities and unique abilities threaten to detach you from reality. Beware of overdoing your "visits" to these esoteric worlds. You must be firmly grounded in reality and everyday life in order to preserve your sanity and continue to function; you must also find a common language with the "mere mortals" around you, even if they do not share your spiritual gifts.

Do not become arrogant or indulge in delusions of omnipotence. Beware of setting yourself up as a miracle-worker. Remember that you are only a human being, and as such, your powers are limited. Be humble and act with generosity of spirit so that you may take full advantage of your qualities, both for your own benefit and for that of humanity.

12. The numerological analysis of number 7 according to cosmic vibrations

Despite the fact that the number 7 is considered to be a lucky number in some circles, its pure and basic meaning is not that at all. On the seventh day, all activity halted, and the universe rested from its labor. Consequently, the number 7 is associated with solitude and withdrawal.

The number 7 is represented and symbolized by a triangle next to a square, or a triangle on top of a square.

Number *8*

1. The numerological analysis of number 8 according to the traditional

approach known as "the numerology of Agricola"

Number 8 people are strong, practical, bright, imaginative, intense, and blessed with a great deal of creative energy. They are dreamers and have a tendency toward melancholy. They are trustworthy, they will never betray a trust, and they carry out all their commitments. They are willing to sacrifice a great deal for their loved ones. They are impressive and charming individuals, but sometimes have difficulty expressing affection and feelings.

Number 8 people are very ambitious and will try to take advantage of any opportunity to get ahead. They are interested in money and social status, and are willing to work hard in order to attain their goals. They are able to reach positions of power and authority. They are individualists by nature, but readily adjust to new situations and are in fact able to achieve good results through conventional channels. They are responsible and self-disciplined, and are blessed with the ability to overcome failure and disappointment without requiring support and assistance from others. They are interested in history and the arts, respect tradition, and admire individuals who excel professionally. They are usually lawyers, business people, politicians, scientists, and writers.

In love, they are faithful and devoted, and need constant confirmation of their partner's loyalty. They are horribly jealous, though try to free themselves of this tendency. They cannot stand the fact that their partner shows an interest in someone else, a trait which frequently leads to separation. These individuals tend to get involved in fights and arguments concerning the principle of things. They are not especially concerned with order and cleanliness, though they are willing to adapt themselves to their partner's habits. They love comfort and luxury, but are ready to make do with less. They are willing to cooperate with relatives, but will not make a special effort to do so. Although these people seem to be balanced, cold and distant, they are actually prone to extreme moodiness. They are gentle, generous, and sympathetic to the weak and suffering.

Eight symbolizes destruction and renewal, threat and promise. This is the number associated with material success and involvement in earthly matters. The financial situation of number 8 people may fluctuate sharply. The dual nature of this number is apparent in its symbol: a circle on a circle. Number 8 symbolizes earthly matters, success and conquest as opposed to failure and retreat. At the same time, it also symbolizes eternity. In the Christian numerical symbolism, eight represents life after death. A horizontal 8 is the mathematical symbol for infinity ∞.

2. The numerological analysis of number 8 according to characteristics of love and sexuality

Number 8 people may justifiably claim that numerologists have been unfair to them in giving them a reputation for having frigid temperaments... to the extent that they are all but seen as "walking refrigerators."

And it is actually untrue. Number 8 people enjoy a good, strong sexual nature, and are frequently quite impressive.

Their potent sexuality is often wasted, since they tend to do everything slowly, in a considered manner, after researching, examining, and testing, and when they are finally ready... the door slams in their face!

Number 8 people find it difficult to understand that love and sex are a realm where more is hidden than revealed. They act as if they are following a recipe, and will never add salt to the soup before adding pepper...

It is therefore important to differentiate between his attempt to feel his way, and his conquest, as there is a tremendous difference between these two stages in his life.

Likewise, for their own good, it is important for number 8 people to understand the difference between the means and the end – for their own good.

3. The numerological analysis of number 8 according to astro-numerology

This refers to those born on the eighth, seventeenth or twenty-sixth days of the month.

Saturn, actually symbolized by the inverted symbol of Jupiter, represents Chronos, that is, the time factor. However, this does not refer to the narrow definition of time, chronological time, but rather to a broader understanding of time – cyclical time. Each cycle begins and ends, and that is indeed Saturn's nature.

Therefore, Saturn sets limits for man. He provides us with a starting point... and an end point! The combination of laws dictated by the planets (destiny) with Saturn (time's steady rhythm) creates the framework of human life.

It is important to understand that Saturn provides us with the opportunity to reach our destiny – but not without a struggle.

Saturn revolves approximately three times during the course of one's life – about 28 years per revolution (a human generation, in fact) – thereby enabling the individual to reach his destiny in three stages: finding himself, identifying with society, and identifying with higher reality, the cosmos.

Number 8 symbolizes this path both by the actual shape of the number, as well as by its location on the numerical axis. The number combines material, spiritual, and infinite consciousness.

Number eight is crucial when analyzing a long-term numerological chart.

4. The numerological analysis of number 8 according to vowels

You are a forceful person with the ability to work hard in order to achieve your desires. Perfection and success in life are important goals for you. You do not always listen to the advice of others, even when you are sure of their good intentions. You have the traits of a lone wolf. You believe in yourself, and yourself alone, and find it difficult to cooperate with others. You have managerial abilities and could easily oversee a large staff or control extensive projects. For this reason, you should learn to include others in your decision-making and seek their assistance as a means of maximizing your success. Not only would you benefit from the help they can provide, but you would also be able to take advantage of their advice, guidance and experience. At times, you unintentionally hurt people's feelings. Be aware of this and learn to respect others.

You seek mental, physical, and spiritual balance. This is the essence of your search in life, and those around you seem to think that you will not rest until you experience the pleasure of wholeness. To this end, you are prone to engage in extraordinary activity – a broad spectrum of activity, both mental and physical. You are able to begin your day very early in the morning, swim for an hour before work, rush off to work, attend a lecture on spiritual matters afterwards, and end your day by cleaning the house thoroughly. Usually, you reach a breaking point and find yourself falling on your nose, unable to function until you have renewed your energy. Learn to control your urge to experience everything, so that you will be able to reach the equilibrium you want.

5. *The numerological analysis of number 8 according to consonants*

Even if you have not yet achieved a position of financial status, there is no doubt that you are on the right path.

You are willing to invest many hours of work in order to attain the coveted success, which for you is mainly in the material realm.

You are gifted with excellent management skills and enjoy not only sounding important, but also looking so. You love expensive suits, sparkling jewelry, designer ties and matching cufflinks. Fancy clothes and nice things are *de rigueur* for you.

People tend to respect you even before they get to know you. Making an impression is very important to you; however, you also know how to be gentle, considerate and attentive to the needs of others.

If you are in charge of a staff of workers or if there are people who are subordinate to you, they never hesitate to come to you with their problems. They know that despite your impressive, high-power facade, you will be sympathetic.

You radiate charm and know how to captivate those who come into contact with you, whether at work or at play. Learn to give more prominence to your inner nature, as you have a lot to offer.

Your inner aspects will help tone down your highly external side, and you will only benefit from such a move.

6. *The numerological analysis of number 8 according to the date of birth*

There is fulfillment of your wishes, objectives, desires and aspirations. You have the power to make things happen. You establish yourself in positions of authority, high status and success, but you tend to ignore the fact that your relentless race to attain your objectives may disturb those around you. Try to avoid using power as much as possible, and assume positions of moderation wherever possible. Aggressiveness will get you nowhere. Avoid violent situations. Be assertive to the appropriate extent.

Money is all-important to you. You are willing to work hard and at various things, as well as do the impossible in order to accumulate as much money as possible. You view the possession of great wealth as a means of achieving all your objectives in life – from material things to the other aspects of life in which money plays a role, such as the ability to hold powerful positions of authority, control, and respect.

However, there are also those who, although money is important to them, do not consider it their greatest achievement. If you are among these individuals, you find it more meaningful to be socially accepted as a person with high status, to be treated with respect, and to wield authority. Money is merely the means for achieving these goals, or the benefit that accompanies high rank.

Some number 8 people consider money to be of equal importance to other things in life. If you hold this view, you will always find yourself somewhere in the middle – not highly influential, not with superior status, and not wealthy.

You are destined to face difficult situations which at times involve quite a struggle. These situations are merely intended to help you develop, learn lessons and seek the equilibrium between the physical and the spiritual.

The amount of effort will determine the extent of success in life. Great efforts will bear fruit, and determination and perseverance will pay off in the end.

Absolute truth is the important thing in your life. If you follow the path illuminated by truth and do not deny it, you will learn to be sincere, both with yourself and your surroundings; you will certainly enjoy positive results.

Your skills are an excellent starting-point, and you must learn to take advantage of them in the most positive manner possible.

The integration of material and spirit suits you. You must take advantage of the knowledge and experience you have accumulated throughout your life in order to utilize them correctly.

7. The numerological analysis of number 8 according to the birthday

This is the time to achieve the goals and objectives that you have aspired to for a long time. It is an excellent time to realize your aspirations and implement grandiose plans. Do not miss this opportunity; take full advantage of it!

Your material situation will be good during this period, and you will be successful in business or at work. Expect a promotion or unusually positive feedback from your superiors.

At the moment, the timing of whatever you do is crucial. It will affect the course of things.

Do not let peripheral issues distract you. Act without undue hesitation so that you do not miss this golden opportunity.

Avoid extravagance, and be careful how you spend money. Your desired objectives may require the investment of a hefty sum of money. Consider carefully if it is actually worth your while, and plan your steps judiciously.

8. The numerological analysis of number 8 according to the nine-year cycle

This year should have good results: joint investments, successful joint business ventures, or the possibility of receiving a large loan from a friend, which will lead you to handsome, unprecedented profits.

Give backing and support to those around you who require it. Be sensitive and listen carefully to the needs of the people close to you. Try to assist them in any way possible. You too will benefit, as *you* will also be able to lean on *them* in times of need and receive their support. Give of yourself in a broader forum as well. You will become aware of the contribution you have made to others and it will create in you a sense of satisfaction and a feeling that you are doing the right thing.

9. The numerological analysis of number 8 according to the

partnership number

The partners must find the balance between them. Usually, they are pulled in different directions. They must try to maintain a relationship in which they are able to find a common ground.

Money is valuable and important in life, but no more important than the need to give expression to the soul. The couple must not let their lives become a continuous quest for material things, nor should they become acquisitive; having said this, they should not turn their lives into a constant search for spiritual fulfillment.

10. The numerological analysis of number 8 in raising children

This child is quite aggressive and requires restraint at an early age. If his parents do not pay due attention to the early stages of his development, the child might develop violent behavior patterns. Because of his active nature, he must constantly be in motion, and this is exhausting for the parents. However, they must not give up and allow the child too much freedom. They have to set limits and explain to him that we need order if we are to live in the world; he must take into account the limitations imposed by his environment. He knows how to express himself well and must therefore be encouraged to give vent to his tensions and aggressiveness in various ways. To do so, parents must be aware of the child's favorite means of expression. It might be in speech, the arts – such as music or painting – or sports. If the child is allowed to express himself freely and without coercion through one of these means, his aggressiveness and violent behavior are likely to decrease. This type of child needs a lot of warmth and love. Physical contact is important for sound emotional development for any child, and all the more so for this child.

If he learns to respect himself and his family, he will grow up knowing how to respect others and be sensitive to their feelings.

11. The numerological analysis of number 8 according to the first and

last name

Your main strength lies in your ability to connect the material and the spiritual. Material success is very important to you and it is the yardstick according to which you measure yourself and your achievements. You are not afraid of hard work and are willing to make a great effort in order to attain your life goals.

Persistence is your key word and you do not give up easily, even if you do not succeed immediately. You appreciate efficiency, and when you begin a particular project, you work with great devotion. It is very difficult for you to withstand life's temptations. For this you need iron discipline. On the other hand, although the temptations are very attractive to you, you resist them admirably.

You have a tendency to exaggerate. When describing a situation either verbally or in your imagination, you tend to blow it out of proportion. This is a dangerous trait and may harm your credibility. It is crucial that you be aware of it and try to stick to reality as closely as possible.

You are impatient to reach a higher social status and become wealthy, but remember that the spiritual realm is just as important to you as the material world is.

For people such as yourself, the pursuit of wealth usually ends in disappointment. In the end, even if you achieve your goals and become wealthy, you will always feel that you have missed out on something.

You are never completely satisfied with what you have. If you feel guilty about the fact that your accomplishments at work are coming at the expense of your family, it is a sign that you should slow down. Be aware of your needs. This is the only way you will avoid malaise and a feeling of missed opportunities.

12. The numerological analysis of number 8 according to cosmic vibrations

The number 8 represents the beginning of new processes following the conclusion of previous processes.

* The material symbol, which consists of two squares one on top of the other.

* The spiritual symbol, which is the figure 8 itself lying on its side.

Number *9*

1. The numerological analysis of number 9 according to the traditional

approach known as "the numerology of Agricola"

Number 9 people are decisive, active, courageous, and have excellent leadership skills. The number 9 indicates control, initiative, determination, vocation, and intuition. These people inspire others and exert a strong influence over them. They are successful, and their achievements are often brilliant. They go through alternate periods of successive victories and times of difficulty and conflict. They have a quick, clear understanding, a great imagination, lofty ideals and a genuine love for humanity. However, their ambition to improve the lot of humanity and change the world is inclined to make them insensitive to the needs and feelings of those close to them. They may be outstanding, often in an amusing manner. They can be amusingly different, instinctive, and open to unanticipated bursts of inspiration. They are impulsive, dreamers, and romantics, and are occasionally gifted with ESP, especially telepathy.

Number 9 people are physically attractive, and usually have extraordinary artistic talent. Many are excellent painters, sculptors, writers, musicians, scientists, teachers, and doctors.

When it comes to love, they are honest, trustworthy, impulsive and faithful. They do not tend to be jealous, but are very difficult if their jealousy is aroused. They are able to compromise in good spirit; even when they do share someone else's opinion, they do not bear a grudge. Generally, they try to fulfill their spouse's wishes in an entirely unselfish way. They have a great appreciation for friendship, feel a deep bond with old friends, and are very keen on a good relationship with family members. However, they will not stand for any interference from their relatives.

The symbolic significance of number 9 is its position as the last and highest of the single-digit numbers. It indicates spiritual achievement, courage, a highly developed sense of self, and humanitarianism. It triples the power of number 3 (3 x 3 = 9). When 9 is multiplied by another factor, the sum of the numerals of the product always equals 9:

(9 x 2 = 18; 1 + 8 = 9) (9 x 3 = 27; 2 + 7 = 9)
(9 x 4 = 36; 3 + 6 = 9), and so forth.

This number represents totality. Human pregnancy last nine months, 360 degrees constitute a circle (3 + 6 + 0 = 9). It is a mystical number. It is said: "The ancient teachers of the occult knew that in the 'higher enumeration,' the number 9 represents the name of God, consisting of 9 letters." Kabbalists believe that the name of Adam (the first person, representing all of humanity) reveals that man is God manifested in flesh. God is the source of all things, just as the numbers 1 to 9 are the root of all things, and all other forms originate and develop from them.

Similarly, the Gematria (the numerology of Hebrew letters) of the name Adam is 45. (The Hebrew letters Aleph=1; Daleth=4; and Mem=4; a sum total of 45), and the sum of those two numerals equals 9 (4 + 5 = 9.) The number 5 appearing in the Gematria of the name Adam represents the physical side of the human being. The number 9 represents his superior spirituality.

2. The numerological analysis of number 9 according to characteristics of love and sexuality

Number 9 people constitute a problem for numerologists who base their readings on astrology. They express the energy of number 1, balance number 6, and are ruled by the masculine planet Mars. Numerologists know this well, but when attempting to interpret the characteristics of number 9 regarding love and sexuality, they discover that reality is different than the theories related to the stars.

Numerology has to view the sexuality and love of number 9 in a different way. On the one hand, these people have a potent sexuality resulting from the product of 3 x 3, and on the other, they are very loyal, due to the fact that this number ends the first cycle of numerological numbers.

And indeed, in spite of the fact that number 9 lacks the emotion of love, the combination of sexuality and fidelity compensates for their characteristic lack of feeling. They are considerate of their partners, see their needs to be as important as their own, and are attentive to every complaint or difficulty in the relationship. Seen in this light, number 9's path with regard to love and sexuality will be better understood.

3. The numerological analysis of number 9 according to astro-numerology

This refers to those born on the ninth, eighteenth or twenty-seventh days of the month.

Today, the symbol of Mars is recognized as the symbol of male sexuality. There is no doubt that Mars serves as a central planet with regard to the birth chart.

In mythology, Mars was Venus' lover. He is also the god of war. To a certain degree, the expression, "All's fair in love and war," originates in this duality.

There is also no doubt that Mars is a male factor – even more so than the sun – in view of the fact that he focuses mainly on the earthly expression of masculinity – war, and love of the body!

But we must remember that Mars closes the circle of planets in that it represents the transformation of the sun's power in opposition to Venus, but with an earthly expression.

In numerology, this situation is much more apparent. Although 9 is an important number, it is not a significant factor in the numerological chart. The reality of 9 actually presents us with the earthly expression of number 1.

4. The numerological analysis of number 9 according to vowels

Your good-hearted and even over-generous nature may cause others to take advantage of you. While you need constant displays of love, at the same time you are not always able to give love in return.

You have a highly developed artistic nature, and are an artist at heart. You are gifted with good hands, and even if you are not a painter or sculptor, you most certainly excel in another form of artistic expression, such as carpentry. You always know how to fix things at home and have an extraordinary ability to improvise. You are original, possessing a broad perspective that is unique and different. You invariably know how to take junk from the street and make something useful out of it, producing things that others would not even have dreamed of.

You strive to be knowledgeable and always try to read a lot. You are capable of reading an entire newspaper, including the gossip columns, just to be up-to-date on "what's happening." It is important for you to stick to reality. You do not allow yourself to float off to faraway worlds or simply to dream that your wishes will come true – just so that no one can ever accuse you of imagining unrealistic things.

Remember that you will always find yourself with both feet firmly planted in reality, because that is who you are. Therefore, you may occasionally allow yourself to let go and even delude yourself with dreams. If you do not dream, how will you fulfill your hidden desires?

5. The numerological analysis of number 9 according to consonants

You are gifted with the ability to adjust to any circumstances. You are in your element not only amongst dignitaries, intellectuals and the wealthy, but also amongst the simplest and poorest of folk. You get along with everyone. You do not make great demands on life, since you are easy to please and satisfied with what you have. You are resourceful and can make the best of even the worst conditions. You enjoy reading and are educated and knowledgeable.

A hopeless romantic, you enjoy writing poetry for your beloved and bringing her flowers. With regard to love and romance, you have no qualms about anything. Whatever you feel you must do to win your beloved's heart, you will do. Even if others view these actions as demeaning, you would never view them as such. You are blessed with a loving and warm heart, and enjoy giving of yourself.

Do not overdo it, at the risk of becoming a nuisance or a burden to your loved one.

You have the qualities of an artist. If you get involved in the arts, you have a good chance of achieving impressive results.

6. The numerological analysis of number 9 according to the date of birth

This indicates bringing ideals to fruition. Your beliefs and ideals provide you with a broad perspective of life. You do not focus on details at the micro level, but rather see things at the macro level.

Your ability to differentiate between the wheat and the chaff enables you to have an overall view of life. You are not limited to or caught in standard molds.

You are able to develop creative and original thinking, and can consequently contribute greatly to human development.

Your power manifests itself in every aspect of your essence. It speaks of spiritual elevation, considered and responsible talk, and courage. There is danger in repressing these energies in the body, as they might erupt uncontrollably. It is crucial to utilize these energies and know how to control them.

Your potential ability is endless.

You would be wise to focus on the needs of your immediate surroundings, then expand the circles gradually until you encompass the whole of humanity with your positive energies.

7. The numerological analysis of number 9 according to the birthday

This is a time of completing circles, bringing things to a close. During this period, tasks that you have undertaken will reach a successful conclusion. You are completing a cycle and ending another chapter in your life; however at the same time, you are beginning a new cycle and a new chapter. This process of closure energizes you for a new beginning.

There may be separations from people you love, and renewed connections with others, or you might make new friends.

In addition, there may be crises – either material or spiritual. In any case, you will emerge strengthened, which will help you to cope with different kinds of crises during the next stages in your life.

8. The numerological analysis of number 9 according to the nine-year cycle

This is the right year to finish things you began in the past. It is very possible that the efforts you are making at work, business or in the home at the moment will only bear fruit in a number of years. However, you will certainly see results.

9. The numerological analysis of number 9 according to the

partnership number

The partners must be open to others. They must learn to love other people rather than just themselves. Giving to others and the desire to give of themselves as much as possible is likely to lead them to the realization of the immense inner powers with which they have been blessed, and to elevate their relationship to a higher spiritual plane.

10. The numerological analysis of number 9 in raising children

Number 9 children take an interest in anything that comes their way. They are inquisitive. They are capable of taking things such as watches, etc. apart in order to see how they work. They are energetic, and, the same time, very sentimental. They must be supported during times of pressure and not be expected to cope on their own, particularly during the first stages of life. Emotional support is likely to strengthen them considerably.

They are aware of the plight of others, and are interested in and fascinated by the pain in the world. Their sense of social justice is highly developed, and even at a tender age they know how to give to others. They inquire about the reasons for life's injustices and problems.

These children will grow up to be concerned citizens. If their sensitivity toward others is brought to the fore and not suppressed by the environment, both they and society will benefit when they mature.

11. The numerological analysis of number 9 according to the first and

last name

This indicates the possibility of attaining wholeness. This wholeness manifests itself through the suppression of the desires of the moment, and by helping others, listening to their problems and being good to them. It is crucial that you learn to make others and their needs a top priority in your life, placing them before yourself.

You must learn to rise above petty concerns, and show nobility and generosity of spirit, even when in difficult and unpleasant situations. You are on a high spiritual level – one that demands commitment. Conserve your strength for the future, because you are not allowed to throw in the towel, even in the most difficult of times. The pleasure and satisfaction that you derive from life are not those enjoyed by most people. The better you treat others, reaching higher spiritual levels on your way, the more fulfillment you will feel by experiencing happiness and peace.

12. The numerological analysis of number 9 according to cosmic vibrations

The number 9 represents the maximum amount of perfection that a person can attain.

The perfection of the number 9 is expressed, among other things, in its ability to conceal itself among the rest of the numbers, and it does not know that it is in their vicinity. However, despite these expressions of modesty, the number 9 is capable of flaunting its uniqueness in front of the rest of the numbers and it does not know that they are in its vicinity.

$1 + 9 = 10 = 1 + 0 = 1$
$2 + 9 = 11 = 1 + 1 = 2$
$3 + 9 = 12 = 1 + 2 = 3$
$4 + 9 = 13 = 1 + 3 = 4$
$5 + 9 = 14 = 1 + 4 = 5$
$6 + 9 = 15 = 1 + 5 = 6$
$7 + 9 = 16 = 1 + 6 = 7$
$8 + 9 = 17 = 1 + 7 = 8$
$9 + 9 = 18 = 1 + 8 = 9$

Despite this number 9 is capable of exhibiting its uniqueness. This can be seen when it is multiplied by any single-digit number, as we see below:

$1 \times 9 = 9$
$2 \times 9 = 18 = 1 + 8 = 9$
$3 \times 9 = 27 = 2 + 7 = 9$
$4 \times 9 = 36 = 3 + 6 = 9$
$5 \times 9 = 45 = 4 + 5 = 9$
$6 \times 9 = 54 = 5 + 4 = 9$
$7 \times 9 = 63 = 6 + 3 = 9$
$8 \times 9 = 72 = 7 + 2 = 9$
$9 \times 9 = 81 = 8 + 1 = 9$

Day-to-Day Prediction

"What is in store for me?"

By means of numerology, you can know what the foreseeable future holds for you on a daily basis. All you have to do is get up in the morning, think of the question, "What is in store for me?" and ask your lucky number what's happening!

Fast, simple, and effective!

You determine your lucky number using two pieces of data... and with luck!

First of all, think of your first name – the one people call you – in terms of the principles of numerology. Give each letter its numerological value according to the table below, add up the numbers, and reduce each total until you get a single-digit number, from 1 to 9. However, if the letters add up to 10, 20, 30, 40, and so on (that is, a number ending in zero, write down 0 in the appropriate place).

A-J-S-1
B-K-T-2
C-L-U-3
D-M-V-4
E-N-W-5
F-O-X-6
G-P-Y-7
H-Q-Z-8
I-R-9

For instance, let's take the name "Karen":
$2 + 1 + 9 + 5 + 5 = 22 = 2 + 2 = 4$

The numerological value of the name "Karen" is 4.

Write the number down on the right side. (See page 94.)

Next, add up the numbers of the date upon which you are asking the question, according to the same principles – month, day of the month, and the two last digits of the year (tens and units).

For instance, let's take the date 10.29.00 (October 10, 2000):
$1 + 0 + 2 + 9 + 0 + 0 = 12 = 1 + 2 = 3$

The numerological value of the date is 3.

Write the number down on the left side.

Now, look at the square below, close your eyes, and place your finger on the square. Let's say that your finger touched the number 8.

1	2	3
4	5	6
7	8	9

Write the number you chose in the middle. If you place your ifnger outside of the squaqre or on a line between two numbers, so that it is impossible to know which number is indicated, write down 0.

3	8	4

What you have finally come up with is a three-digit number. Now find this combination (384) in the book, and see what your future holds, according to the art of numerology.

Read the sentence that appears beside the combination of numbers you reached (see the above examples), and act accordingly. Sometimes the sentence will be clear and decisive, and sometimes it will contain vague clues only.

You can write down all the numerological predictions for, say, a week on a sheet of paper – one prediction per day. At the end of the week, or later on, examine the predictions, and ask yourself if they actually came true – all or most of them. (See page 174.)

100   Keep your eyes peeled, and be cautious! This combination of numbers indicates that it is dangerous for you on the roads.

101   This combination of numbers indicates that a year of many opportunities is in the offing.

102   This combination of numbers indicates that you can expect failure in a competition with others.

103   This combination of numbers indicates that you will soon meet someone who will have a great influence on your life.

104   Large bodies of water constitute a threat to you. This combination of numbers says that it is not advisable to go for a sea cruise or to sail in a boat...

105   You must work toward putting your plan into practice. This combination of numbers indicates that there will be strong opposition to a plan that you present.

106   This combination of numbers indicates that important information is on its way to you.

107   This combination of numbers indicates that you can expect joy from a happy marriage.

108   Pay attention to fulfilling your obligations properly. This combination of numbers says that it is advisable to restrain your enthusiasm and initiative!

109　This combination of numbers indicates that people will abuse your generosity. Don't lend money!

110　This combination of numbers indicates that you must take action and not procrastinate.

111　This combination of numbers indicates that there is a great deal of uncertainty in the immediate future. You are advised to think seven times before making any decision.

112　This combination of numbers indicates and predicts something bad. This can be prevented by taking counter-measures.

113　This combination of numbers indicates that you will be out of luck, but not seriously, for a short time. A business enterprise will only be slightly successful.

114　This combination of numbers indicates that there is a chance of economic success and prosperity. You will meet a stranger who will become a close friend.

115　This combination of numbers indicates that a wealthy person can expect a heavy financial loss. A poor person can expect an improvement in his financial situation.

116　This combination of numbers is a warning against illness and disease, which can be avoided by taking the correct precautions in advance.

117　This combination of numbers indicates that there are evildoers in your vicinity. Be sure of the facts before accusing anyone.

118　This combination of numbers indicates that your deeds are of little importance and short-lived. Better be safe than sorry!

119　This combination of numbers indicates that there is a period of happiness and beneficial change. Marriage is a good idea during this time.

120   This combination of numbers indicates that a loss is in the offing. You should exercise a great deal of caution in everything concerning financial transactions.

121   This combination of numbers signifies that happiness and prosperity are just around the corner.

122   This combination of numbers indicates that there are many opportunities in various fields. Keep your eyes open! Beware of a change in luck.

123   This combination of numbers indicates a trip to a distant country. New friends will influence you. There will be adventures and new enterprises.

124   This combination of numbers indicates that you can expect bad luck! Many unseen enemies are conspiring against you.

125   This combination of numbers indicates that there will be a change for the better in your circumstances. You will receive money from an unexpected quarter.

126   This combination of numbers indicates that there will be a brief period of losses and bad luck, followed by a long period of success in everything you do.

127   This combination of numbers indicates that you will receive good tidings from distant relatives who you've never heard from before. They will be coming home (to you) very soon!

128   This combination of numbers is good for people who are starting new enterprises. Success will accompany them from the outset.

129   This combination of numbers is a warning of danger and problems, especially to those people who are traveling by ship or plane to a distant country.

130   This combination of numbers indicates that a devoted and loyal friend is influencing your life. Don't ignore his advice!

131   This combination of numbers indicates a speedy recovery from an illness or accident, but you must take the required precautions to ensure a permanent recovery.

132   This combination of numbers indicates a successful, prosperous, and carefree marriage.

133   This combination of numbers indicates that you will have good luck. You will be successful in anything to do with games of chance.

134   This combination of numbers indicates that there will be a change, and chances are that it will be for the better. Take every opportunity that crops up in your path!

135   This combination of numbers indicates that an investment this year will yield good profits. There will be an unexpected windfall.

136   This combination of numbers indicates that you can expect bad luck! Don't undertake new enterprises during the current month.

137   This combination of numbers indicates a new friendship, but not always a good one.

138   This combination of numbers indicates that a guest you expected will be delayed. You will be invited to visit a friend of the opposite sex.

139   This combination of numbers indicates that women can expect good luck... and men can expect bad luck. They must refrain from any kind of gamble.

140   This combination of numbers indicates that efforts to uncover secrets will be partially successful. You won't like everything you find out.

141   This combination of numbers indicates a definite improvement in your affairs. There is a chance of a promotion or a rise in status.

142　　This combination of numbers advises you to be on the alert! You can expect a threat of danger from people you meet on a daily basis.

143　　This combination of numbers indicates that the big success will occur within the time span of the coming year.

144　　This combination of numbers indicates that a disease threatens you or someone dear to you. Don't take any unnecessary risks.

145　　This combination of numbers indicates that lovers have cause to fear a quarrel or heartbreak. The danger is already approaching!

146　　This combination of numbers indicates that soon you will hear from an old friend with whom you lost contact a long time ago.

147　　This combination of numbers indicates that you should refrain from getting embroiled in lawsuits or bureaucratic problems. You can expect a loss.

148　　This combination of numbers indicates that wealth and happiness await you in the near future.

149　　This combination of numbers indicates that you are about to "star" in a scandal. See that you don't provide any concrete grounds for this black cloud.

150　　This combination of numbers warns you not to trust others too much. True friends might reveal themselves to be false friends.

151　　This combination of numbers indicates that you will have a lot to do in various fields. There will be trips abroad and a great deal of business enterprises.

152　　This combination of numbers says: Don't despair if the situation looks gloomy and hopeless – it will improve, and there is light at the end of the tunnel.

153   This combination of numbers indicates that your fears are groundless! Stand up for yourself and you will discover that your fears were unjustified.

154   This combination of numbers indicates that a long journey awaits you. Be careful of air travel, because there is danger lurking there!

155   This combination of numbers indicates that you can expect a new, good friendship, and it will be of great significance in the future.

156   This combination of numbers indicates that you can expect to move house. Only numerous "anchors" can prevent the move.

157   This combination of numbers indicates satisfying love affairs. A good marriage is on the horizon.

158   This combination of numbers indicates that you can expect success… but don't set too much store by this, since everything is liable to collapse!

159   This combination of numbers indicates that money is on its way to you, apparently by inheritance. Make sure to invest it wisely.

160   This combination of numbers says that you should take care not to gossip about people close to you, otherwise friendship will become hostility.

161   This combination of numbers indicates that danger awaits you – but in the end, following difficulties, everything will work out for the best.

162   This combination of numbers indicates that you will have luck in a gamble or a high-risk investment – but make sure not to go overboard.

163   This combination of numbers indicates that there will soon be a change, but it is not clear whether it will be good or bad. Pay attention to the path you have to choose!

164   This combination of numbers indicates that good tidings are on their way by mail. There is a chance that you will change environment or atmosphere.

165   This combination of numbers indicates that you will receive a tempting offer. Work fast, otherwise you'll miss the opportunity.

166   This combination of numbers indicates that you will soon encounter difficulties. Seek help and advice from your friends.

167   This combination of numbers indicates that financial embarrassment awaits you. Don't gamble, and don't take risks.

168   This combination of numbers indicates that you will receive an offer to make a lot of money – but it involves a lot of pitfalls! Don't take it.

169   This combination of numbers advises you to beware of what you say in anger. The consequences are liable to be fraught with disaster for you.

170   This combination of numbers indicates that good things await people who love nature and the natural life – good health and a good life are on the horizon!

171   This combination of numbers indicates that you are about to discover a new field of interest that will occupy you in the distant future.

172   This combination of numbers advises you to refrain from gambling or investing in the near future, since your financial situation is on the verge of collapse.

173   This combination of numbers indicates that you will receive an announcement that will be of great financial significance to you in the near future.

174   This combination of numbers indicates that someone close to you has irksome problems. Help him, and together you will overcome the obstacles.

175   This combination of numbers indicates that there will be quarrels and conflicts, but you will not be affected, and your future will be rosy.

176   This combination of numbers indicates that you can expect a meeting with a person who will influence your life in a revolutionary way – for the better!

177   This combination of numbers indicates that a new opportunity will crop up for you – grab it at any price, since success is guaranteed!

178   This combination of numbers advises you to make the most of every opportunity if you are in a creative field, since success awaits you around the corner.

179   This combination of numbers advises you to be wary of disappointments in business or gambling. The odds are patently against you.

180   This combination of numbers indicates that there will be a pleasant change in your life. You will be compelled to leave home for a short time.

181   This combination of numbers indicates that there will be a change in luck! Death may occur, unless counter-measures are taken.

182   This combination of numbers indicates that the coming year will be good to you, especially financially.

183   This combination of numbers indicates that you should not gamble in business or finances. A wise investment will bear fruit.

184   This combination of numbers indicates that unexpected tidings will bring a mixture of sorrow and joy.

185   This combination of numbers indicates that an unstable situation can be expected. Difficult circumstances require a great deal of effort and repair.

186   This combination of numbers indicates that you can expect changes in the realm of home and family and economic problems in the coming years.

187   This combination of numbers indicates that a problem may crop up, mainly as a result of the interference of a relative. Avoid this!

188   This combination of numbers indicates that your great expectations are liable not to be realized. Don't undertake spurious ventures.

189   This combination of numbers indicates that a lot of money will reach your hands. The prosperity will continue for a brief period.

190   This combination of numbers indicates that anyone who is in a bad situation can expect good things. The change will rectify the situation.

191   This combination of numbers indicates that you can expect good results from a business transaction. You will have to leave home for a protracted period.

192   This combination of numbers indicates that a relative will suffer loss and damage, and you will be the one who is expected to mend the damage.

193   This combination of numbers says that a disease is expected, which can be avoided. A long journey by train or car is in the offing.

194   This combination of numbers indicates that you will be the recipient of happiness and love. There will be a marriage in the family or among your friends.

195   This combination of numbers warns of hitches, especially in the field of business. Be careful, and weigh things up well before each decision.

196   This combination of numbers indicates that you will receive money. A broken friendship will be revived.

197   This combination of numbers advises you to beware of the person who sticks his nose in your personal affairs: even if he seems like a friend, he will stab you in the back.

198   This combination of numbers indicates that you can expect good or bad, and for that reason you have to be especially cautious.

199   This combination of numbers indicates that the person who travels by land or by sea will be immune from danger.

200   This combination of numbers is not very significant, but if it recurs, it is extremely significant!

201   This combination of numbers advises you not to try anything out of the ordinary. The coming months are not too favorable.

202   This combination of numbers indicates that whoever is involved in art or some other form of creativity will succeed. People in trade, commerce, and practical professions – watch out!

203   This combination of numbers indicates that young people will go off on new adventures, while older people will stay at home and reminisce.

204   This combination of numbers indicates that caution will benefit your affairs, since the coming month will bring nothing but loss.

205   This combination of numbers advises you to avoid lawsuits – you are liable to lose and pay out a lot of money!

206   This combination of numbers indicates that you can expect to encounter obstacles and massive opposition to an economic enterprise, so it would be better not to get into it for the time being.

207   This combination of numbers indicates that you can expect problems in taking care of your family, but this will eventually come right.

208   This combination of numbers indicates that an event that is very influential in your life will occur. Protect yourself from disease that can prevent your success.

209   This combination of numbers says that if you are involved in a competitive field, try to compete now, since your chances are good.

210   This combination of numbers advises you to stay away from high places or dangerous roads, since a serious accident is foreseen.

211   This combination of numbers indicates that the color red will bring you good luck. Wear red whenever you can.

212   This combination of numbers indicates that important tidings are expected. See that you are always available.

213   This combination of numbers indicates that business affairs are on the upswing. Don't miss opportunities.

214   This combination of numbers indicates that poor health is threatening your life. Stay away from crowded places.

215   This combination of numbers indicates that a long trip will be proposed. Weigh it up well – this trip is liable to jeopardize your relationships.

216   This combination of numbers indicates that you must not believe everything you hear. Naïveté leads to foolish actions.

217   This combination of numbers indicates that Thursday is a day of bad luck for you. Don't start anything new on a Thursday.

218   This combination of numbers indicates that a great deal of happiness awaits you in natural surroundings. Go out into nature and allow yourself to revel in it.

219   This combination of numbers indicates that you must not follow an artistic inclination. Be a person of action – otherwise you will get into difficulties.

220   This combination of numbers indicates that good luck is in the offing, but take care not to be selfish. You are capable of realizing all your aspirations.

221   This combination of numbers indicates that interesting news will reach your ears, and it will bring about a change in your luck.

222   This combination of numbers indicates a potentially disastrous trip. Confusion and embarrassment will have an effect on you.

223   This combination of numbers indicates that every thing, name, or place beginning with the letter G has a negative significance for you.

224   This combination of numbers indicates that love and good luck will come into your life thanks to a new acquaintance that you will make in a new city.

225   This combination of numbers indicates that there is a danger of fire or a conflagration. This is a one-off situation that will pass.

226   This combination of numbers indicates that you can expect an important meeting in the near future. Don't miss it or be late – otherwise you will lose out.

227   This combination of numbers advises you to be careful when you are holding a knife or sharp object. A serious injury is foreseen in the near future.

228   This combination of numbers indicates that there is a danger of theft, mugging, or damage to property. Be careful – and see that you have the relevant insurance!

229   This combination of numbers indicates that anyone involved in trade can expect good things. There will be prosperity and opportunities for making a lot of money.

230   This combination of numbers advises you to control your stormy temper, since an outburst is liable to cause the breaking of good, important ties.

231   This combination of numbers indicates that someone far away... is near to you. Good or bad news will arrive.

232   This combination of numbers indicates that written material will affect your life. Be careful not to interpret what is written incorrectly.

233   This combination of numbers warns you not to try to defraud and deceive others, since in the end, it will backfire very badly on you.

234   This combination of numbers indicates that your hopes and aspirations are not solidly founded. Do what you can to base your aspirations soundly.

235   This combination of numbers indicates that jewelry and expensive objects will bring bad luck. Hide your wealth until the bad luck goes away.

236   This combination of numbers indicates that contacts with others will bring good luck in the evening only. Exercise is essential for your health.

237   This combination of numbers indicates that the sea and love are linked in your life, and everything that links the two will lead to a great deal of happiness.

238   This combination of numbers indicates that you can expect a separation and break-up soon. A broken heart will soon be mended.

239   This combination of numbers says that caution and alertness are recommended in everything concerning domestic matters. You can expect success and large profits in the field of business.

240   This combination of numbers indicates that it is advisable to keep your private affairs a secret... especially from your friends! The advice of a friend will mislead you.

241   This combination of numbers indicates that if you have artistic
talents, you must exploit them fully. Artisans must work very
cautiously.

242   This combination of numbers indicates that you will meet an
extremely influential patron who intends to help you without
seeking gain for himself. Follow his advice.

243   This combination of numbers indicates that someone you consider
a friend does not deserve your trust. You have the power to
overcome people who wish you ill.

244   This combination of numbers indicates that there is danger in
taking risks or in gambling. Don't act impulsively.

245   This combination of numbers indicates that there is a difficult
period ahead, but it will be followed by a period of wealth and
prosperity.

246   This combination of numbers indicates that you can expect a
change in your life – a wedding in the family circle. You will
begin climbing the social ladder.

247   This combination of numbers indicates that you will meet a friend
who traveled far away. You can expect a lengthy trip to a distant
place.

248   This combination of numbers indicates that this is the time for
sport and trips for young people. They are advised to go on long
trips.

249   This combination of numbers means that you must not worry
about your bad situation today; things will turn out fine
unexpectedly.

250   This combination of numbers indicates that there will soon be an
important birth in your family or in the family of a close friend.

251   This combination of numbers indicates that this is a good time for thinkers or people with scientific talents. Fame and a good reputation await them on their path.

252   This combination of numbers says that if you've been getting bad signals, pay heed to the warning.

253   This combination of numbers indicates a superfluous legal or bureaucratic embroilment. It is a warning to mend your ways.

254   This combination of numbers warns you not to make money at your friends' expense, since this turns friendship into rivalry.

255   This combination of numbers advises you to invest time in studies and planning. The day when you can prove your talents is approaching.

256   This combination of numbers indicates that religion and belief play an important role in your life. Don't deny religious conduct.

257   This combination of numbers indicates that there is a promise of a wedding hidden here, but there is no certainty that the promise will be kept.

258   This combination of numbers indicates that you can expect a brief period of success and prosperity, but you have to remember that this situation will change rapidly.

259   This combination of numbers warns you not to rush and not to risk your money, since bad luck is liable to lead to a big loss.

260   This combination of numbers says that it is advisable for you to make a change in your lifestyle, especially in everything concerning your occupation and livelihood.

261   This combination of numbers indicates that an evil sign is threatening your life. Make sure that you are cautious for the coming month.

262   This combination of numbers indicates a chance of making a great deal of money from an unexpected source.

263   This combination of numbers indicates that you can expect personal problems in the area of home and family. Patience and tolerance will prevent a major crisis.

264   This combination of numbers indicates that you will meet a lot of people you've never met before, but you have to be careful in your choice of new friends.

265   This combination of numbers indicates that joy and happiness will fill your heart and home. Be careful not to relate to important things too lightly.

266   This combination of numbers indicates that a long-term aspiration will be realized if you devote all your efforts to this aim.

267   This combination of numbers indicates that difficulties and rivalries will stand in your way, but ultimately you will reach your goal.

268   This combination of numbers indicates that you have an ambitious nature. Take care that ambitiousness does not drain your strength.

269   This combination of numbers indicates that wealth and happiness await you, both at home and when you go out.

270   This combination of numbers indicates that you can expect failure in a competition with others. Next year, you will have great success.

271   This combination of numbers indicates that you will have a long and satisfying life, but every now and then problems will occur.

272   This combination of numbers indicates that there will be a mixture of joy and sorrow in your life and your family's life, but there will be more joy than sorrow.

273   This combination of numbers indicates that you will receive good tidings from a distant source of which you were previously unaware.

274   This combination of numbers indicates that you will soon be asked to sign an extremely important document! Get legal advice immediately!

275   This combination of numbers indicates that you can expect a period of success and prosperity. Don't change any of your plans.

276   This combination of numbers indicates that success in the field of sport or art will lead to the establishment of a sound economic status.

277   This combination of numbers indicates that economic issues are at the center of attention. Seek new and profitable investments.

278   This combination of numbers indicates that somebody is plotting to harm you, but you will outwit him.

279   This combination of numbers indicates that extramarital affairs will not affect your marriage this time.

280   This combination of numbers indicates that among your friends, there are many enemies. Choose new friends for yourself, and get away from enemies.

281   This combination of numbers says that it is not advisable to go on a cruise or sail in a boat. Large bodies of water constitute a threat to you.

282   This combination of numbers indicates that if you act intuitively, it is a sign that you can expect great success.

283   This combination of numbers advises you to act cautiously in everything concerning livelihood and money. Hard times are approaching and money will be short.

284   This combination of numbers indicates that the person who is involved in a creative occupation will be successful. Speedy success will lead to fame and great honor.

285   This combination of numbers says that there is a sign that indicates a change for the better. There will be a substantial improvement in your financial situation.

286   This combination of numbers indicates that you can expect a tempting proposal to change your lifestyle – don't miss the opportunity!

287   This combination of numbers indicates that letters from a friend will bring glad tidings – a wedding is on the horizon.

288   This combination of numbers indicates that there is only a small chance that your aspirations and wishes will be realized in the coming months.

289   This combination of numbers says that it is advisable for you to beware of the malice of one of your relatives, otherwise you will suffer a severe financial setback.

290   This combination of numbers is a sign that opens the gates to success. However, make sure that you are not gullible.

291   This combination of numbers indicates that the coming years will be years of happiness and wealth. Take advantage of these happy years.

292   This combination of numbers indicates that everyone who works in the creative field can expect mild success in the fields of prose or poetry.

293   This combination of numbers indicates that if you are interested in aviation or anything that is connected to the air, success is guaranteed.

294   This combination of numbers indicates that temporary changes and hitches stand in your way. There is more suffering than happiness during this period.

295   This combination of numbers indicates that very soon you will be repaid, and your efforts will be properly rewarded.

296   This combination of numbers indicates that if love and romance have been lacking in your life, a refreshing change will take place.

297   This combination of numbers indicates that in anything to do with love and romance, this is a period of blooming and renewal.

298   This combination of numbers indicates that the coming year will witness the realization of most of your aspirations – but not all.

299   This combination of numbers indicates that you have overcome many obstacles, but other obstacles still await you.

300   This combination of numbers indicates that anyone who is involved in music and creativity can expect a change of great positive significance.

301   This combination of numbers indicates that your expectations will be realized, but only partially.

302   This combination of numbers indicates that an enemy of yours is posing as a friend, and is liable to bring disgrace and shame onto your head.

303   This combination of numbers indicates that you have many dreams and aspirations, but only a few of them are in fact realized.

304   This combination of numbers indicates that a period of trials, suffering, and sorrow is expected, followed by a reward of happiness and joy.

305   This combination of numbers indicates that a letter will arrive, warning you of a false friend. This is a serious matter that you should not take lightly.

306　　This combination of numbers indicates that if you are a person who spends a lot of time in the streets, stay at home. If you are a person who sits at home, get out into the streets.

307　　This combination of numbers indicates that sorrow and grief will disappear from your life very soon, to be replaced by a period of love and happiness.

308　　This combination of numbers indicates that you can expect a warning sign concerning a fall... This fall can be avoided by thinking before you act.

309　　This combination of numbers indicates that talented people will fail while attempting to fulfill their expectations. People who lack talent will succeed.

310　　This combination of numbers advises you to increase your efforts to attain success, since this is your year of success.

311　　This combination of numbers advises you to be careful of entering into new partnerships. In all probability, the damage will be greater than the benefit.

312　　This combination of numbers indicates that you live way beyond your means. Your aspirations shape your life path.

313　　This combination of numbers indicates that there are financial advantages on your path to success, but you do not make enough effort to attain that success.

314　　This combination of numbers says that a misunderstanding with a person close to you will lead to a real conflict. Only time can heal the breach.

315　　This combination of numbers indicates that a loyal friend, whom you have not fully appreciated up to now, will bring a great deal of happiness into your life.

316　　This combination of numbers indicates that hard work will lead to great wealth and honor.

317   This combination of numbers is a sign that heralds honor and wealth for anyone who is connected to the medical profession.

318   This combination of numbers indicates that extremely significant social occasions will determine your immediate future.

319   This combination of numbers is an ancient sign with one meaning: "Marry in haste, repent in leisure."

320   This combination of numbers indicates that a significant change at this moment will lead to disaster in the short run.

321   This combination of numbers indicates that a new area of interest will open up to you. Partnership will lead to the path to success.

322   This combination of numbers indicates that you can expect success in business... and total destruction in your love life!

323   This combination of numbers says that it is advisable to abstain from the company of strangers, because they will have a bad influence on your life.

324   This combination of numbers indicates that for anyone who is connected to the establishment or to highly influential organizations, the coming year will not be favorable!

325   This combination of numbers indicates that the near future is overcast and gloomy. Danger lurks in the financial realm.

326   This combination of numbers indicates that people who are involved in writing or communications can expect success... after a number of failures.

327   This combination of numbers indicates a long trip to a distant country. When you return home, you will be rich in money and experience.

328   This combination of numbers indicates that there are brilliant chances in the near future, marred only by family and domestic conflicts.

329　　This combination of numbers says that it is advisable not to sign any document. Someone is scheming to exploit your innocence.

330　　This combination of numbers indicates that this is a good time for actors and musicians. These arts are favored during the coming year.

331　　This combination of numbers indicates that a period of wealth and prosperity lies ahead. Courage will put you onto the correct path.

332　　This combination of numbers indicates that there will be a change in your place of residence, and every change will be for the better.

333　　This combination of numbers indicates that you can expect gifts and legacies. Enjoy surprises.

334　　This combination of numbers indicates that in five months' time, a new period of happiness for you and the members of your household will begin.

335　　This combination of numbers indicates that it is advisable to take advantage of the opportunity that has presented itself to you. Success and advancement are foreseen.

336　　This combination of numbers indicates that it is dangerous for you on the roads. Keep your eyes peeled, and be cautious!

337　　This combination of numbers indicates that a long-lost friend will contact you, and his advice will benefit you enormously.

338　　This combination of numbers indicates that wealth and profit are on their way to you… but not from the source on which you had pinned your hopes.

339　　This combination of numbers indicates that young people are significant, and instructs them to make an effort at work and in their studies.

340　　This combination of numbers is a warning against getting involved in crime because of the bad influence of a fly-by-night "friend."

341   This combination of numbers indicates that a lack of consideration on your part will lead to a split with a friend, and you will be the one to pay the price in the future.

342   This combination of numbers heralds the good news that everything that has been flawed in your life up till now will change for the better in the coming year.

343   This combination of numbers forecasts great success, provided that it recurs twice in a row.

344   This combination of numbers indicates that soon you will be asked for financial help – and it will be a very good idea for you to refuse!

345   This combination of numbers indicates that you are desperate to accomplish your objectives… but the chances of success are small.

346   This combination of numbers is of importance to artists and actors at the beginning of their careers.

347   This combination of numbers is very important for women, and forecasts good health.

348   This combination of numbers indicates that in the near future, you will be the victim of malicious gossip, but you will not suffer any real damage.

349   This combination of numbers indicates that a risky financial investment will bear fruit in the distant future.

350   This combination of numbers warns you not to trust your friends' advice too much. Act according to your own discretion.

351   This combination of numbers indicates that the plans you made will collapse and disappear. Don't despair – in the end, everything will work out.

352   This combination of numbers indicates that you can expect a bitter disappointment following news you receive at home.

353   This combination of numbers engenders a great deal of hope, especially in the heart of a sick person.

354   This combination of numbers indicates that if you want to change your occupation, now is the time to do so.

355   This combination of numbers indicates that ambition and hard work will enable you to overcome all the difficulties.

356   This combination of numbers says that it is advisable to accumulate financial resources to the best of your ability... soon you will have the opportunity to make a successful investment.

357   This combination of numbers indicates that an obdurate and malicious enemy will bother you, but ultimately you will get the better of him.

358   This combination of numbers is a warning against long journeys, since danger lurks on the roads.

359   This combination of numbers indicates that there is danger in anything to do with fire. Caution and attention will prevent the danger.

360   This combination of numbers indicates that old troubles are finally laid to rest, and a period of happiness is on the threshold.

361   This combination of numbers indicates that a great passion for adventure is soon going to be satisfied.

362   This combination of numbers indicates that a great deal of money will arrive from an unexpected source. There will be legal or bureaucratic problems.

363   This combination of numbers indicates that you can expect plots and intrigues to be hatched against you. You will need assistance in counteracting them.

364   This combination of numbers indicates that you can expect an improvement in your economic and social status. You are the target of a great deal of jealousy.

365   This combination of numbers indicates that you can expect a year filled with achievements, but not necessarily a year of happiness.

366   This combination of numbers advises you to take full advantage of your capital in order to realize your aspirations.

367   This combination of numbers indicates that times will improve. There will be a period of happiness.

368   This combination of numbers indicates that the immediate future is bright and promising, but heavy clouds are gathering on the horizon.

369   This combination of numbers indicates that malicious enemies are trying to erode your status.

370   This combination of numbers indicates that soon you will receive a business proposal that you would be well advised to decline.

371   This combination of numbers indicates that good sense in matters of money and livelihood will be beneficial to you and the members of your household.

372   This combination of numbers indicates that a good opportunity is presenting itself to you. Seek professional advice before making a decision.

373   This combination of numbers brings good news to poor, weak people, but is insignificant to the wealthy.

374   This combination of numbers is a warning against a serious mistake in matters of the heart and love.

375   This combination of numbers says that it is advisable to take advantage of every opportunity that is offered to you, since now is your time to succeed.

376   This combination of numbers indicates that you can expect a brief period of sorrow and grief, but the sun will brighten the near future.

377   This combination of numbers says that it is advisable to refrain from conflicts with relatives and friends, otherwise you will reach the point of a domestic crisis.

378   This combination of numbers indicates that you can expect glowing encounters with friends, accompanied by a long trip to a foreign country.

379   This combination of numbers indicates that you must take precautions in matters of money and property. The chances of losing are greater than the chances of making a profit.

380   This combination of numbers indicates that people will abuse your generosity. Restrain your generous impulses. Don't lend money!

381   This combination of numbers foretells black and evil. It is a serious warning when the sign recurs.

382   This combination of numbers indicates that bad news will arrive in a letter. A problem that you have ignored will pop up again.

383   This combination of numbers indicates that you can expect a change in the home and family scene. It could be a good change, but it could be a bad one!

384   This combination of numbers heralds a great deal of money that will reach your wallet.

385   This combination of numbers indicates that suffering, loss, and troubles lead to a long absence from home.

386   This combination of numbers indicates that if you are not married, one of your friends will make you an offer you can't refuse.

387   This combination of numbers indicates that an act of theft or robbery will damage your property. Do whatever you can to prevent this evil.

388   This combination of numbers indicates that you can expect danger, but you will not know the source of it.

389   This combination of numbers indicates that you can expect damage to your property that will result in substantial financial loss.

390   This combination of numbers indicates that it is advisable to be careful of a group of friends who are plotting your downfall.

391   This combination of numbers indicates that it is advisable to be practical and energetic in material affairs, and stay away from affairs of the heart.

392   This combination of numbers indicates that troubles and problems will become a thing of the past, and a shining light will illuminate your life.

393   This combination of numbers indicates that hard work and effort will result in a lot of money.

394   This combination of numbers indicates that a new enterprise will lead to honor and financial profit.

395   This combination of numbers indicates that a new friend will come into your life, bringing... good or evil, who knows!

396   This combination of numbers indicates that fulfilling your obligations meticulously will create a firm basis for your status.

397   This combination of numbers indicates that there will be a sharp and enjoyable about-turn in your relations with the opposite sex.

398   This combination of numbers indicates little love and a lack of romance – a happy marriage is the tried and tested cure!

399   This combination of numbers indicates that by means of talent and a great deal of diligence, you will attain the status you deserve in society.

400   This combination of numbers says that you shouldn't pin too much hope on your friends. Rely on your own abilities and actions only.

401   This combination of numbers indicates that you can expect a long life, but your path will be characterized by ups and downs.

402   This combination of numbers indicates that you will receive news from a distant place, and this will cause a fundamental change in your lifestyle.

403   This combination of numbers indicates that there are many problems, mostly personal ones, ahead. You can expect to lose friends and status.

404   This combination of numbers indicates that you will be involved in an important and happy marriage... of another couple, unfortunately!

405   This combination of numbers indicates that legal and administrative problems are ruining your life.

406   This combination of numbers indicates that unseen enemies are causing problems in your home and family life.

407   This combination of numbers indicates that a lot of activity lies ahead of you. A long journey is not always such good news for you!

408   This combination of numbers indicates that a plot is being hatched against you. Employ caution and wisdom to prevent this evil.

409   This combination of numbers indicates that a huge plot is being hatched behind your back. Keep your private affairs absolutely secret!

410　　This combination of numbers indicates that you can expect a change in your place of residence. There is also a possibility of a change in profession or job.

411　　This combination of numbers indicates that one of your most precious aspirations will soon be realized... but not in the immediate future.

412　　This combination of numbers is important for sick or disabled people, because a complete recovery is within their reach.

413　　This combination of numbers indicates that a married person can expect long-term happiness. A single person can expect a period of stagnation or wretchedness.

414　　This combination of numbers indicates that you will be rewarded for your serious, on-going efforts by a prestigious job or honorable status.

415　　This combination of numbers indicates that it is not advisable to pin too much hope on the realization of your aspirations.

416　　This combination of numbers indicates that you can expect an unpleasant incident. Avoid gambling and taking risks.

417　　This combination of numbers indicates that you can expect financial profit. Your luck will improve in the near future.

418　　This combination of numbers indicates that there is a threat of serious problems and illnesses. Seek help and support among the members of your family.

419　　This combination of numbers indicates that a change in atmosphere and place of residence will bring good luck and happiness into your life.

420　　This combination of numbers indicates that enemies are plotting against you, but everything will turn out in your favor.

421   This combination of numbers indicates success and achievements, mainly in your professional field.

422   This combination of numbers heralds a great deal of success and honor for anyone who is involved in the musical and instrumental field.

423   This combination of numbers says that it is advisable to refrain from sending letters to friends, since the things you say will be interpreted with a negative twist.

424   This combination of numbers is a promise of an unexpected gift of money.

425   This combination of numbers indicates that there will be strong opposition to a plan that you present. You must work toward putting your plan into practice.

426   This combination of numbers says that it is advisable not to interfere in other people's domestic affairs, since ultimately you are the one who will be hurt!

427   This combination of numbers indicates that help in time of need will come from an old, long-forgotten friend.

428   This combination of numbers says that you must not build your life around the expectation of receiving a particular piece of news, because a serious disease is delaying everything.

429   This combination of numbers is bad news. You will not realize your aspirations or your plans.

430   This combination of numbers is a sign of great success for people who are involved in art and other creative fields.

431   This combination of numbers indicates that an aspiration from a long time ago is about to be realized. It is a sign of substantial financial gain.

432   This combination of numbers says that it is advisable to be calm and confident, and problems will pass with minimal damage.

433   This combination of numbers is excellent and presages success for people who deal with words, especially those involved with the theater (playwrights).

434   This combination of numbers is a threat to happiness, especially that of people who are involved in marriages of convenience.

435   This combination of numbers indicates that business failure and substantial financial losses can be expected. These can be reduced by means of caution and thought.

436   This combination of numbers indicates that manual laborers can expect a slow but real improvement. Researchers and scientists will make an important discovery.

437   This combination of numbers indicates that with the help of a stranger who has been unknown to you until now, you will substantially improve your social status.

438   This combination of numbers indicates that it is advisable for you to conduct yourself cautiously in all the steps you take, since a great danger is threatening you.

439   This combination of numbers indicates that a close friend will come into a large amount of money (from a legacy), and you will enjoy the leftovers of his table.

440   This combination of numbers indicates that if you want to invest money, consult an expert! This sign predicts a "fall" for you.

441   This combination of numbers indicates that a disease is threatening your family. With professional help, you can prevent it – or cure it.

442   This combination of numbers indicates that happiness is coming your way – probably related to marriage.

443   This combination of numbers heralds wealth and happiness for married women, but bad things for men.

444   This combination of numbers indicates that anyone who is involved in trade can expect a period of great success.

445   This combination of numbers says that it is advisable to be cautious in all your deeds. Only caution will prevent mistakes and failures.

446   This combination of numbers indicates that there will be problems in your love life. Try to overcome the obstacles.

447   This combination of numbers indicates that you will have huge expenses. Help will come from an unexpected source.

448   This combination of numbers indicates that a big change is about to occur, and you will acquire a great deal of life experience from it (but not more than that).

449   This combination of numbers indicates that there is a great deal of logic in your aspirations and plans, but you are not doing enough to realize them.

450   This combination of numbers can be interpreted in two ways: good in the economic realm, bad in the domestic realm.

451   This combination of numbers indicates that the immediate future will be full of bitter tears, but later on, the sky will become clear.

452   This combination of numbers indicates that you can expect long journeys, mainly to do with your job and profession.

453   This combination of numbers says that it is advisable to be patient and considerate in your dealings with others, and they will treat you in the same way.

454   This combination of numbers indicates that there is a lot of hypocrisy in the way people around you relate to you. Be careful, otherwise you will be badly hurt.

455   This combination of numbers indicates that the immediate future holds nothing but trouble for anyone who is inclined to gamble without limits.

456   This combination of numbers indicates that you must take precautions against everything to do with fire. Do whatever you must in order to prevent a disaster.

457   This combination of numbers indicates that you can expect a year of success and happiness both at home and at work.

458   This combination of numbers is good news for young people. Their dreams will soon come true.

459   This combination of numbers heralds a happy family event… but not necessarily concerning you directly!

460   This combination of numbers foresees good health, a long life, and a stable marriage.

461   This combination of numbers says that it is not advisable to pin too many hopes on a plan that is unsound.

462   This combination of numbers indicates peculiar incidents that augur ill, but their influence will diminish in a short time.

463   This combination of numbers says that it is advisable to look after yourself well, since there are many purveyors of evil in your vicinity.

464   This combination of numbers indicates that there are signs of change for the better in your affairs, but this will only happen if you take an active part in them.

465   This combination of numbers indicates that happiness and sadness will occur in tandem over the next few years. Marriage will bring happiness and prosperity.

466   This combination of numbers indicates a long sojourn in a distant country, at the end of which the person will return home and live happily.

467   This combination of numbers indicates that a person who opposes you and works against you will eventually turn out to be a true friend.

468   This combination of numbers indicates that you can expect wealth and gain in the future. A large inheritance is on its way to you!

469   This combination of numbers indicates that you receive various strange offers, but you must weigh each one up very carefully.

470   This combination of numbers warns you to be tight-lipped about everything concerning affairs of the heart and of the pocket.

471   This combination of numbers indicates that good luck and bad luck appear as a pair. You will make the correct choice if you are cautious every step of the way.

472   This combination of numbers indicates that rare opportunities for success are in the offing. Hold onto the situation with both hands!

473   This combination of numbers indicates a bad year for everyone involved in the law and legal affairs. Watch out for financial failures.

474   This combination of numbers says that it is advisable to be careful of dangers connected to fire or water. Check your path carefully before setting foot on it.

475   This combination of numbers says that it is advisable to refrain from borrowing money or possessions, since you will be unable to return it.

476   This combination of numbers indicates that a relative or a sick friend will benefit greatly from your presence beside them.

477   This combination of numbers indicates that while you are fulfilling all your obligations, you will gain gratitude and profit for yourself.

478   This combination of numbers indicates that many obstacles will occur in your life, but you will overcome all of them.

479   This combination of numbers indicates that although you are full of doubts and fears about the future, it looks like you will succeed in realizing your aspirations.

480   This combination of numbers indicates that there will be a family embroilment. A bad piece of advice you were given is damaging to you.

481   This combination of numbers indicates that a surprising chance for success and wealth has presented itself. Act wisely, otherwise you will miss the opportunity.

482   This combination of numbers indicates that you can expect good health, and overcome diseases or accidents.

483   This combination of numbers indicates that there will be an economic crisis... but luckily it is only temporary.

484   This combination of numbers says that it is advisable to be cautious in your dealings with strangers! They covet your property and are liable to hurt you.

485   This combination of numbers is significant only for a creative artist, and informs him of difficulties in creative expression.

486   This combination of numbers indicates that a risky gamble or investment will bring you a nice profit.

487   This combination of numbers foretells happiness and prosperity for anyone who got married this month!

488   This combination of numbers indicates that a chance meeting brings good news... or a threat to your life.

489   This combination of numbers indicates that your efforts for advancement in your workplace will not bear fruit in the near future.

490   This combination of numbers indicates that you can expect a change in your place of residence in the near future. In the more distant future, there will be a move to another city.

491   This combination of numbers indicates that it is advisable to continue with the plan in which you are involved at the moment, since the chances for success are rising all the time.

492   This combination of numbers indicates that you trust your friends... and your friends are the ones who will bring about your downfall! Trust yourself only.

493   This combination of numbers indicates that you can expect professional advancement concurrently with personal problems at home.

494   This combination of numbers says that it is advisable to cancel all your appointments in the coming week, because nothing good will come of them.

495   This combination of numbers indicates business complications that will continue for a long time. You will emerge rich in experience, and poor in pocket!

496   This combination of numbers indicates that a problem with your home or family will affect your future seriously.

497   This combination of numbers indicates that people whom you trust are betraying you, but you will foil their plots.

498   This combination of numbers indicates that you will encounter rejections and delays along your path. However, patience will enable you to overcome all of them.

499   This combination of numbers indicates that the coming year will bring you success if you take advantage of the opportunities that have been offered you.

500   This combination of numbers indicates an inevitable and substantial financial loss. This will be made good and compensated for only in the distant future.

501   This combination of numbers indicates that you are faced with an important business decision. Seek professional advice.

502   This combination of numbers heralds good health and great happiness... and slight progress in the economic realm.

503   This combination of numbers indicates that news, or a sign of life, will arrive from a person about whom you have heard nothing for many years.

504   This combination of numbers foretells that you will reject your present lifestyle, and will adopt a different one.

505   This combination of numbers foretells advancement for people who work in a government or bureaucratic institution.

506   This combination of numbers indicates that a big plan will not be profitable... you're building a house of cards!

507   This combination of numbers indicates that an inclination for travel and adventure will lead to a change in your occupation.

508   This combination of numbers is bad news for entrepreneurs or gamblers. General collapse is imminent!

509   This combination of numbers says that it is advisable to refrain from ties with a close friend who is liable to cause you disaster.

510   This combination of numbers indicates that in the coming months, you will experience great happiness, and your financial affairs will also improve.

511   This combination of numbers tells you… not to trust anyone! A so-called friend will be detrimental to you.

512   This combination of numbers indicates that you will acquire an honorable standing thanks to your moral values.

513   This combination of numbers says that it is advisable to be careful of accidents, since the sign hints that you will be hurt.

514   This combination of numbers indicates that your troubles are coming to an end – good or bad? Who knows?

515   This combination of numbers indicates that an investment in anything concerning property or real estate will lead to a surprising and immediate profit.

516   This combination of numbers indicates that your aspirations have been halted by an obstacle that will be removed only in the distant future.

517   This combination of numbers says that it is not advisable to flaunt your wealth, since this will tempt fate.

518   This combination of numbers indicates that you can expect serious and deep emotional problems that only love can cure.

519   This combination of numbers indicates that the future will be favorable to you, and that money will solve many of your problems.

520   This combination of numbers says that it is advisable to make every effort to complete your plans, since this is the time to implement them.

521   This combination of numbers indicates that somebody is sniffing around your love relationships with evil intent, and will hurt you.

522   This combination of numbers augurs well, but in contrast, there are people who want to do you harm.

523   This combination of numbers indicates that you can expect journeys or a protracted vacation, at the end of which there will be a terrible hitch.

524   This combination of numbers indicates that you can expect disappointments and losses that only time can put right.

525   This combination of numbers indicates that there will be a significant change in your life, an improvement in your financial situation.

526   This combination of numbers advises you not to interfere in your friends' private affairs, otherwise you yourself will become a problem for them.

527   This combination of numbers indicates that you can expect a sea voyage. There is a chance that you will immigrate to another country.

528   This combination of numbers indicates that you can expect a romantic liaison in the near future, but it has nothing to do with marriage.

529   This combination of numbers says that it is advisable to restrain your enthusiasm and initiative! Pay attention to fulfilling your obligations properly.

530   This combination of numbers indicates that your friends' advice will benefit you. Beware of hidden enemies.

531   This combination of numbers indicates that all those who are involved in creativity can expect a successful year. Be careful of accidents while traveling.

532   This combination of numbers indicates that in the future, your luck will take a turn for the better... but until then, you will have to operate on your own.

533   This combination of numbers says that it is advisable not to take risks with yourself, especially not risks concerning your health.

534   This combination of numbers indicates that a financial loss, or a loss of property, is expected. Be careful and watch out...

535   This combination of numbers indicates that young people, and even children, are guaranteed success in difficult exams.

536   This combination of numbers advises you to be careful of gambling or of risky investment, since the coming years will be difficult for you.

537   This combination of numbers indicates that there is danger of an accident or drowning at sea. Safeguard your health and do a lot of exercise.

538   This combination of numbers indicates that danger threatens you, but you can do nothing to prevent it.

539   This combination of numbers says that it is advisable not to worry about the future... at the moment you do not have the means to change it for the better!

540   This combination of numbers indicates that ambition and energy will not bring about the desired results.

541   This combination of numbers indicates that ups and downs in your love life are liable to break up your relationship.

542   This combination of numbers indicates that a long-forgotten aspiration from long ago will suddenly be realized in an unexpected manner.

543   This combination of numbers says that it is advisable to refrain from ties with the opposite sex during the coming week, otherwise you will get in huge trouble.

544   This combination of numbers indicates that your work will be very well received, and will advance your status in your workplace.

545   This combination of numbers indicates that problems in the romantic realm can be solved by means of common sense.

546   This combination of numbers says that it is not advisable to embark on new adventures, since they are liable to end in disaster.

547   This combination of numbers says that it is not advisable to sign any legal document, although pressure will be brought to bear on you to do so!

548   This combination of numbers is excellent for anyone who is involved in competitive sports. Sporting achievements will lead to an improvement in your status.

549   This combination of numbers indicates that you have very few true friends, but among them, there is one who will be of benefit to you.

550   This combination of numbers indicates that a disease is threatening your health. Caution will prevent the disease and its attendant damage.

551   This combination of numbers indicates that a quarrel and a break-up with a loyal friend will hurt your soul in the near future.

552   This combination of numbers indicates that you rely too much upon your talents. Reality will show you the error of your ways.

553   This combination of numbers indicates that bad luck will lead to a substantial financial loss from which you will only recover in three years' time.

554   This combination of numbers indicates that an unexpected inheritance is on the horizon... but there is no guarantee that it will reach you.

555   This combination of numbers indicates that problems and difficulties lead to suffering. The help of a relative brings relief.

556   This combination of numbers indicates that your financial situation is shaky. Beware of taking desperate measures in the economic sphere.

557   This combination of numbers indicates that effort and energy invested in work are not properly rewarded.

558   This combination of numbers indicates that the loss of friends or relatives perturbs you for a long time.

559   This combination of numbers indicates an imminent danger, but does not show you exactly where its source is or how to protect yourself from it.

560   This combination of numbers indicates that the coming years will be difficult for you, but it is also very difficult to put your finger on a specific event.

561   This combination of numbers indicates that lovers can expect a period of ups and downs. Drawing hasty conclusions leads to sorrow.

562   This combination of numbers says that it is advisable to be careful what you write and especially what you sign. Something written by you can cause you grief in the future.

563   This combination of numbers says that it is advisable to stay away from quarrels in the family circle. A quarrel with a relative will cause you a great deal of chagrin.

564   This combination of numbers indicates that you are trying to acquire a profession to which you are not suited. Find an occupation that suits your life.

565   This combination of numbers says that it is advisable not to worry too much. Superfluous worries will shorten your life.

566   This combination of numbers indicates that something is bothering your conscience and making you depressed. Try to get to the root of the problem and purge yourself of it.

567   This combination of numbers indicates that you need a change. A vacation will be beneficial in advancing your affairs.

568   This combination of numbers indicates that you can expect prosperity and great wealth in the coming months. Large outlays of money are bothering you.

569   This combination of numbers indicates that a secret will be entrusted to you. Keep the secret, otherwise you will lose a friend!

570   This combination of numbers indicates that an aspiration from long ago will soon be realized. Don't let the change alter your lifestyle.

571   This combination of numbers indicates that people below age 35 can expect economic success, while people above age 35 will experience stagnation in their lives.

572   This combination of numbers indicates that people who are excellent professionals can expect a period of wealth and prosperity.

573   This combination of numbers indicates that someone of high standing will use his influence to benefit your affairs.

574   This combination of numbers indicates that an unexpected journey will cause you to change your occupation.

575   This combination of numbers indicates that you will receive glad tidings from someone you seldom hear from, despite his love for you.

576   This combination of numbers indicates that besides "regular" worries, you will have a long and happy life.

577   This combination of numbers indicates that you have to be cautious and alert, otherwise you will be hurt by ill-meaning people.

578   This combination of numbers indicates that many of your aspirations (not all, though) will soon be realized.

579   This combination of numbers says that it is advisable to refrain from speculative financial investments and gambles – otherwise, you will suffer substantial damage.

580   This combination of numbers indicates that there will be a change for the better in matters of love… but only for a short time!

581   This combination of numbers says that it is advisable to continue with your plans. Your chances of success are great.

582   This combination of numbers says that broadening your social circle will lead to advancement and gain in the future.

583   This combination of numbers augurs ill for anyone who is involved in art or other forms of creativity.

584   This combination of numbers indicates that you can expect extensive and enjoyable social activity in the coming year.

585   This combination of numbers says that it is advisable not to leave the borders of your country this year, since an accident will befall you in a foreign country.

586   This combination of numbers is good news for a woman. For a man, it foretells betrayal and difficulties.

587   This combination of numbers says that it is advisable to invest your time and energy in work, otherwise you will miss an opportunity that you will regret.

588   This combination of numbers indicates that in the near future, you will be inclined to pick quarrels. Take care not to cause a split in your family.

589   This combination of numbers indicates good news in everything connected with legacies or lotteries.

590   This combination of numbers indicates that you can expect a dream that augurs ill. Protect yourself from the jealousy of malicious friends.

591   This combination of numbers indicates that many of your aspirations will suddenly be realized... but this will not lead to true advancement in practice!

592   This combination of numbers indicates that you can expect a journey or a protracted absence from your home. There is a chance of a change in your profession or place of work.

593   This combination of numbers advises you to be careful of a treacherous friend who is seeking to hurt you in any way possible.

594   This combination of numbers indicates illness at home or in your family – but there will be a speedy recovery.

595   This combination of numbers indicates that soon you will need to sign a document that will bring you a lot of success in the future.

596   This combination of numbers indicates that a year of great wealth and prosperity is in the offing.

597   This combination of numbers indicates that hard work is the key to success. You were not born with a silver spoon in your mouth!

598   This combination of numbers warns of glitches in the realm of love and romance.

599   This combination of numbers indicates success for people with a literary or artistic bent.

600   This combination of numbers indicates that in the coming months, there will be a change in your status. Be careful in the entrepreneurial field.

601   This combination of numbers says that it is advisable to be extremely cautious – a domestic accident is expected to befall you soon!

602   This combination of numbers warns you not to take risks on the road or on a journey. This sign indicates a traffic accident!

603   This combination of numbers advises you to be careful of fire. Besides that, the coming year will be a good one.

604   This combination of numbers indicates that this year will be a very lucky one for young girls and young women. It will be a danger-filled year for males, however.

605   This combination of numbers indicates that there will not be any changes in your business in the near future, but don't let that stop you.

606   This combination of numbers indicates that a change in occupation or profession is in the offing. Success will be slow, but constant.

607   This combination of numbers advises you to reduce your financial outlay! Your income will decrease substantially.

608   This combination of numbers indicates a painful love affair. In due course, it will have a bad effect on marriage.

609   This combination of numbers indicates that you can expect disappointment, especially in business. Ultimately, you'll come out the winner.

610   This combination of numbers indicates that you are ambitious, but you lack courage and perseverance.

611   This combination of numbers indicates that you can expect a proposal (business? matrimonial?) from someone whom you have little chance of meeting again.

612   This combination of numbers advises you not to tempt fate. Act cautiously, and you will be rewarded.

613   This combination of numbers is good news, mainly for actors and creative people.

614   This combination of numbers foretells financial difficulties. See that you insure your financial future.

615　　This combination of numbers advises you not to place too much trust in your friends' promises. Act courageously in accordance with your own motives.

616　　This combination of numbers indicates that you will be faced with many difficulties, but you have a chance of overcoming all of them.

617　　This combination of numbers indicates that accidents are foreseen for people who are involved in professional sports.

618　　This combination of numbers indicates that your good name will be attacked and besmirched, but ultimately you will emerge unblemished.

619　　This combination of numbers indicates that you are facing a difficult year, but you will overcome all the obstacles.

620　　This combination of numbers indicates that you can expect success in your exams during the coming year.

621　　This combination of numbers indicates that legal problems that are bothering you will eventually bring success and wealth to your home.

622　　This combination of numbers says that you must not fear the future. Do what you can to realize your ambitions.

623　　This combination of numbers indicates that minor difficulties in the business realm can be expected. There is happiness in the spiritual realm and in your love life.

624　　This combination of numbers gives hope to people who are suffering from a serious disease – a surprising recovery is foreseen in the future.

625　　This combination of numbers indicates that you have an unseen enemy who is plotting against you. Act aggressively and stand up to him.

626   This combination of numbers indicates that fire and water will endanger your life or property in the near future.

627   This combination of numbers advises you not to go overboard with plans and aspirations, since your financial means are scant.

628   This combination of numbers says that it is advisable not to gamble and take risks in the coming months. You should especially avoid sea and air travel.

629   This combination of numbers indicates that you have the urge to try your luck on foreign soil. Stay where you are, because you will fail miserably abroad.

630   This combination of numbers indicates that a proposal of marriage (not necessarily to you) seems as if it will change your life – but nothing will happen in the end.

631   This combination of numbers indicates that in the coming year, there will be a significant change in your business arena... but you do not know the direction it will take.

632   This combination of numbers says that it is not advisable to rely on your friends and their advice. Seek the advice of an expert in every single field.

633   This combination of numbers indicates that there is a small chance of an improvement in your status. The more distant future promises a great deal.

634   This combination of numbers indicates that news from far away will present you with a new opportunity.

635   This combination of numbers indicates that you will come into a great deal of money... and not through inheritance.

636   This combination of numbers indicates that your happiness lies in the balance. Stay away from the advice of so-called friends.

637   This combination of numbers indicates that bad news will lead to a particularly painful year.

638   This combination of numbers indicates that a letter containing an invitation will be advantageous to your business.

639   This combination of numbers tells you not to expect rapid success in your business affairs. You will succeed – but at a very slow pace.

640   This combination of numbers indicates that many people will flatter you... but be careful not to turn your back for fear of a knife being stuck in it!

641   This combination of numbers indicates that a year of many opportunities is in the offing. Try and make the most of them.

642   This combination of numbers indicates that a friendship will founder on the rocks... in the future, a more important friendship will come along.

643   This combination of numbers indicates that there will be a period of sorrow and pain that will turn into a period of joy and happiness.

644   This combination of numbers advises you to be careful of any document concerning the law and legal matters. The advice of an expert will be very useful to you.

645   This combination of numbers indicates that people who are involved in the spiritual realm can expect a period of prosperity.

646   This combination of numbers indicates that you can expect a financial crisis as a result of a bureaucratic or legal process.

647   This combination of numbers indicates that self-improvement is in the offing... but carrying it out will be difficult and tedious.

648   This combination of numbers indicates that the time is not right for economic ventures. Continue with what you are doing now.

649 This combination of numbers indicates that troubles will pass. You and the people close to you will have happiness.

650 This combination of numbers heralds a love relationship in your immediate surroundings.

651 This combination of numbers indicates that only with a huge, ongoing effort will you be able to realize your great ambition.

652 This combination of numbers says that it is advisable to beware of a long journey, as it involves many dangers.

653 This combination of numbers indicates that a sudden change (an inheritance?) is expected. You are forced to change your place of residence.

654 This combination of numbers advises you to be careful of disappointments in love... You can expect a lot during the coming year.

655 This combination of numbers indicates that in the near future, you will be involved in organizing a trip, or in a long journey.

656 This combination of numbers indicates that you will lose a close friend, but in his place you will make a new and loyal friend.

657 This combination of numbers indicates that with the help of other people, you will succeed in realizing your big ambitions.

658 This combination of numbers is good news for **old** people... They will receive money from an unexpected source.

659 This combination of numbers is meaningless for men, but indicates a significant change for women.

660 This combination of numbers indicates that becoming acquainted with a stranger will change your future for the better.

661　　This combination of numbers advises you to act with determination, otherwise you will suffer a substantial and painful loss.

662　　This combination of numbers heralds a change. You can expect a long absence from home.

663　　This combination of numbers says that it is advisable to remain cool and patient... although this year will be a year of heavy losses.

664　　This combination of numbers indicates that a quarrel with a relative or a friend will turn out to be a conspiracy against you by someone who hates you.

665　　This combination of numbers indicates that next year, there will be a change in your profession, and in the future, this change will lead to financial gain.

666　　This combination of numbers indicates that a business proposal looks good on the surface... Check it out thoroughly before making up your mind.

667　　This combination of numbers is only important for people in financial distress, warning them against dangerous expenditure.

668　　This combination of numbers warns you not to lose your courage! You have to stand up to attempts to undermine your status.

669　　This combination of numbers indicates that you can expect a long, happy, and healthy life... but you must be careful of pursuing pleasure.

670　　This combination of numbers indicates a significant improvement for people of 30 and over.

671　　This combination of numbers indicates that changes must begin at home or with the family. Take advantage of every opportunity for a change like this.

672   This combination of numbers indicates that in the coming year, you should not get involved in a wedding (not necessarily your own) or in a divorce.

673   This combination of numbers indicates that a person who is older than you will exert a great influence on your life in the future.

674   This combination of numbers indicates that a year of sorrow and pain is in the offing. It is difficult to prevent this on your own.

675   This combination of numbers says that you should not allow a love affair to jeopardize your work or your professional standing.

676   This combination of numbers is vague, to a large extent, and relates to the wedding of a relative (jealousy?).

677   This combination of numbers is good news for people in the musical and instrumental world.

678   This combination of numbers indicates that an inheritance or a cash prize will be delayed for a long time on its way to you.

679   This combination of numbers indicates that you can expect a promotion in your workplace, but its concrete realization entails hard work.

680   This combination of numbers indicates that a gamble or a risky investment is forbidden... You can expect a painful financial loss.

681   This combination of numbers indicates that someone is plotting to harm you. Take the advice of a close friend.

682   This combination of numbers indicates that the coming year will be a mixture of happiness and sorrow, of success and failure.

683   This combination of numbers advises you not to despair, even if it looks like all the odds and facts are against you!

684   This combination of numbers indicates that information you are waiting for is being delayed, resulting in loss and problems.

685   This combination of numbers indicates that you are putting your trust in a new, unknown friend, and this will cost you dearly.

686   This combination of numbers indicates that a great deal of honor is in the offing in the coming years, but in the coming months, difficulty can still be expected.

687   This combination of numbers indicates that extreme and surprising changes can be expected in the business or work field.

688   This combination of numbers indicates that in the coming months there will be a turning point that will mainly affect the realms of home and heart.

689   This combination of numbers advises you not to make hasty decisions without due consideration and consultation.

690   This combination of numbers advises you to be careful with your money and to safeguard it, since you can expect a substantial loss.

691   This combination of numbers indicates that you will soon meet a person who will have a great influence on your future.

692   This combination of numbers indicates that you will face many obstacles.

693   This combination of numbers indicates the break-up of a marriage in your immediate vicinity.

694   This combination of numbers indicates that people with artistic or creative tendencies can expect a year of success and great honor.

695   This combination of numbers indicates that you can expect to make new friends, but don't get too close to them.

696   This combination of numbers advises you to safeguard your health, especially that of your heart, because this year will be difficult and stressful.

697   This combination of numbers indicates that a financial crisis will reduce your status.

698   This combination of numbers indicates that information that reaches you late will prevent you from taking advantage of an important opportunity.

699   This combination of numbers indicates that you risk losing money. Avoid taking chances with money.

700   This combination of numbers indicates that big aspirations lead to small achievements! Match the aspirations to the means.

701   This combination of numbers indicates that love is on a back burner, and the situation will not improve significantly in the future.

702   This combination of numbers indicates that inertia and a lack of initiative are preventing you from making a change for the better.

703   This combination of numbers advises you to be careful of trips to overseas countries, since danger awaits you there.

704   This combination of numbers indicates that wedding bells are in the offing – but not directly for you!

705   This combination of numbers indicates that the death of a distant relative will affect your economic status.

706   This combination of numbers indicates that in the near future, there will not be any real change, but your situation will improve later on.

707   This combination of numbers indicates that you will have a lot of luck in the coming year as long as you rely on yourself.

708   This combination of numbers advises you to keep your eyes open and be cautious. A domestic accident is looming over you.

709   This combination of numbers indicates that you can expect problems at home and in your livelihood, and there is no solution to them on the horizon.

710   This combination of numbers advises you to look after your health, since next year, you will become ill.

711   This combination of numbers indicates that meeting an old acquaintance will change your economic situation for the better.

712   This combination of numbers indicates that a warning from an unknown source will turn out to be of great importance to your future.

713   This combination of numbers indicates that you are not exploiting your talents. Your aspirations must be higher.

714   This combination of numbers indicates that your problems have passed. This will be a successful year.

715   This combination of numbers is a warning against taking risks. An illness can bring you to a halt.

716   This combination of numbers indicates that a business venture will be very detrimental to you.

717   This combination of numbers advises you not to cling to your plans, because the sign indicates failure.

718   This combination of numbers advises you to maintain discretion and secrecy; revealing secrets will harm your goals.

719   This combination of numbers indicates that there will be an improvement in your financial situation that will continue for many years.

720   This combination of numbers engenders hopes of victory in athletes' hearts, but also indicates impending injury.

721   This combination of numbers indicates that the future holds good health and great wealth. There will be new friendships to replace ones that have broken up.

722   This combination of numbers indicates that you will face many difficulties in the near future, but with the help of other people, you will overcome them all.

723   This combination of numbers indicates that you can expect a life of toil, hard work, and effort – but also the promise that you will be suitably rewarded.

724   This combination of numbers tells you not to despair. A bit more effort will realize your aspirations.

725   This combination of numbers indicates that meeting highly influential people will culminate in one of them supporting you.

726   This combination of numbers indicates that you can expect joy from a happy marriage, as well as an ever-improving financial situation.

727   This combination of numbers says that you must not give up... even though there are many reasons for doing so. The future will be better.

728   This combination of numbers indicates that you are about to embark on a long journey. You will change your profession or place of work.

729   This combination of numbers indicates that evildoers are placing an obstacle in your path, but eventually (by means of a lawsuit) you will defeat them.

730   This combination of numbers indicates that you can expect happiness, wealth, and a long life. There will be minor problems that will not disturb your serenity.

731   This combination of numbers indicates that the coming months will be lucky, but you must be careful – the future looks gloomy!

732   This combination of numbers indicates that serious lawsuits are in the offing. Important plans will collapse.

733   This combination of numbers indicates that "friends" are interfering in your life and to your detriment. Act according to your feelings, and not according to your friends' advice.

734   This combination of numbers indicates that you can expect an improvement in your business situation. There will be rapid progress toward realizing your ambitions.

735   This combination of numbers indicates that problems with home and family are in the offing. They will disappear after a short while.

736   This combination of numbers indicates that help from an unexpected quarter will advance your professional standing.

737   This combination of numbers indicates that an elderly friend will die. A new friendship will blossom to make up for it.

738   This combination of numbers indicates that you are about to go on a journey – but there is a lot of danger in it!

739   This combination of numbers indicates unexpected good luck, or a win in a lottery. This is the reward for a brave action in the past.

740   This combination of numbers warns you not to trust anyone who flatters you! Your happiness will be curtailed as a result of the flatterer's actions.

741   This combination of numbers foresees a great deal of luck for people who are connected to a wedding in the coming month... wealth and prosperity.

742   This combination of numbers indicates that a woman, who will have a great positive influence on your life (whether you are a man or a woman), will contact you.

743   This combination of numbers indicates that a change in your place of residence will necessitate a change in your place of work.

744   This combination of numbers indicates that a love affair will be ignited like a flame – and it will go on for a long time!

745   This combination of numbers indicates that you can expect financial difficulties in the near future, and wealth and prosperity in the more distant future.

746   This combination of numbers indicates that someone is sabotaging you. His actions will harm you tremendously.

747   This combination of numbers indicates that fears and anxieties prevent you from implementing a plan that has every chance of succeeding.

748   This combination of numbers is excellent for lovers... their relationship contains happiness and wealth.

749   This combination of numbers indicates that obstinacy and stubbornness are making your life difficult.

750   This combination of numbers indicates that a friend from long ago will re-establish contact with you.

751   This combination of numbers indicates that there will be a substantial change in your lifestyle following an unexpected inheritance.

752   This combination of numbers indicates that glad tidings will come in a letter or telegram. You will enjoy fame and fortune.

753   This combination of numbers indicates that difficulties in a love affair are in the offing. The affair will eventually end.

754   This combination of numbers says that you must not stick your nose into other people's affairs, since ultimately you will be the one who is hurt.

755   This combination of numbers indicates that a close acquaintance will become a friend. This relationship will endure for a long time.

756   This combination of numbers advises you to help the people around you to the best of your ability. In the future, you will need their help.

757   This combination of numbers is a patent warning about money matters or the danger of travel.

758   This combination of numbers indicates that you must take action and not procrastinate. Whoever advises you otherwise is no friend of yours.

759   This combination of numbers indicates that your life is in danger, but there is a ray of light in the otherwise overcast sky.

760   This combination of numbers indicates that you must operate very confidently, with the assistance of your friends and professional advice.

761   This combination of numbers foretells great danger lurking in your path.

762   This combination of numbers indicates that stress, pressure, and difficulties will continue for a few months.

763   This combination of numbers advises you to be careful of investing money because the future holds heavy losses for you.

764   This combination of numbers indicates that you are the target of many complaints and a lot of resentment, and you have to deal with this situation.

765   This combination of numbers indicates that legal or administrative problems are halting the advancement of your affairs.

766   This combination of numbers indicates that you can expect a crisis or a fall in your immediate surroundings, but it is not clear whether or not you will be involved in it.

767　　This combination of numbers advises you to be careful of someone close to you who is conspiring against you. The conspiracy will be exposed very soon.

768　　This combination of numbers indicates that this is the right time to forge ahead. Realize your ambitions and your plans.

769　　This combination of numbers indicates that you can expect good news, as a result of which you will go on a long journey.

770　　This combination of numbers indicates that someone close to you needs your help. Helping him will also benefit you.

771　　This combination of numbers indicates that the situation will be gloomy for a short time, followed by a more successful future.

772　　This combination of numbers indicates that a close friend is causing a conflict. Don't break off your friendship – he is a true friend!

773　　This combination of numbers indicates that there are legal problems and lawsuits ahead, but the future will show that you are in the right.

774　　This combination of numbers is a warning against someone who is posing as a friend – and plans to stick a knife in your back!

775　　This combination of numbers indicates that you cannot expect to succeed in your present place. It would be helpful if you were to move house or change jobs.

776　　This combination of numbers is good for people who suffer from heartache or a disease. The suffering will pass in the future.

777　　This combination of numbers advises you to pay attention to your financial situation, since it is expected to deteriorate.

778　　This combination of numbers advises you to take note that you get into trouble every month, on the 15th or 20th of the month.

779　　This combination of numbers indicates that success is within your grasp, but you are too lazy to make it happen.

780　　This combination of numbers indicates that the ties with an old friend will be renewed – and will change your life.

781　　This combination of numbers indicates that you can expect love, happiness, and romance... but your financial situation will deteriorate!

782　　This combination of numbers is bad for lovers... Love ends, and all that remains of it is a vague memory.

783　　This combination of numbers advises you to stop implementing your plans for at least three months.

784　　This combination of numbers indicates that you can expect an interesting, if somewhat dangerous, adventure in the coming year.

785　　This combination of numbers is a warning not to get involved in anything to do with the law, since the odds are against you this year.

786　　This combination of numbers is not a good sign, especially where health is concerned.

787　　This combination of numbers indicates that you will be successful in the coming months. Take advantage of them for advancing your affairs.

788　　This combination of numbers says that you must not reveal your affairs to other people, because their gossip will be harmful.

789　　This combination of numbers indicates that although you think that you are the victim of bad luck... you and your actions are in fact responsible for the mishaps.

790　　This combination of numbers indicates that you can expect a change in the domestic realm, and probably also in your personal status.

791   This combination of numbers indicates that a gamble or a risky investment will cause a substantial decrease in your capital.

792   This combination of numbers indicates that a year of stagnation is in the offing. Don't be tempted to make hasty financial investments.

793   This combination of numbers indicates that you can expect to suffer in the coming months as a result of the loss of a person or a thing.

794   This combination of numbers indicates that love awaits you in a faraway land.

795   This combination of numbers indicates that you are inclined to be influenced by others, and this influence is distorting your path in life.

796   This combination of numbers indicates that you should think ten times before doing anything. Success depends on profound deliberation.

797   This combination of numbers indicates that news from far-off days raises problems that you wanted to forget...

798   This combination of numbers is good news for all those involved in art or other creative fields.

799   This combination of numbers indicates that the coming year will be successful for anyone who implements his financial plans.

800   This combination of numbers indicates that a marriage can be anticipated in your circle... it may even be yours!

801   This combination of numbers advises you to beware of people posing as friends, as they are about to hurt you.

802   This combination of numbers indicates that an ambition or a plan will be realized, but the gains will not bring you happiness.

803   This combination of numbers is a warning against water and fire.

804   This combination of numbers is a warning against danger that can be avoided.

805   This combination of numbers indicates that financial success resulting from hard work and pooling resources is in the offing.

806   This combination of numbers foretells financial gains alongside problems in love.

807   This combination of numbers is good news for people below the age of 30, and indicates promotion and advancement.

808   This combination of numbers indicates that there is a great deal of danger on the roads in the coming weeks. Your health may be in jeopardy.

809   This combination of numbers indicates that the future is rosy... but numerous dangers threaten you.

810   This combination of numbers advises you not to rely on words and promises... the future holds many disappointments.

811   This combination of numbers indicates that your life will suffer from many shock waves this year, and they are liable to be to your detriment, too.

812   This combination of numbers indicates that a letter will bring you bad news... It will take a year for you to get over the sorrow.

813   This combination of numbers indicates that a friend needs your help... Help him, and you will also benefit.

814   This combination of numbers indicates that evildoers are gathering around you. Keep your eyes open, otherwise you will be hurt.

815   This combination of numbers indicates that wealth and happiness await you in a distant land over the sea.

816   This combination of numbers advises you to steer clear of investments in the coming weeks, since luck will not be on your side during that time.

817   This combination of numbers indicates that domestic problems are in the offing. Take care not to exacerbate a conflict.

818   This combination of numbers advises you not to waste your money, since you will be short of money in the near future.

819   This combination of numbers indicates that danger is in the offing in the coming month.

820   This combination of numbers indicates that you will be faced with an extremely important decision. Seek advice and help from experts.

821   This combination of numbers indicates that health is in jeopardy (particularly children's health). You must take care of your health very thoroughly.

822   This combination of numbers is bad news... Lightning is liable to strike the person who does not protect himself and his home!

823   This combination of numbers indicates that someone you are soon going to meet will try to defraud you.

824   This combination of numbers advises you not to make important decisions in the coming week because your judgment is impaired.

825   This combination of numbers indicates that you will soon meet someone who will have a great influence on your life... Make sure that it is the correct person.

826   This combination of numbers indicates that courage and perseverance will lead to wealth.

827   This combination of numbers indicates that a scandal involving you will be publicized and will be injurious to your standing.

828   This combination of numbers is a warning. Shake off your complacency and get ready for the struggle!

829   This combination of numbers indicates that you can expect a change in status or place of work, but how successful this change is depends on you.

830   This combination of numbers indicates that someone is courting you... but his intentions are not to your benefit.

831   This combination of numbers advises you to prepare for a positive change that will mainly affect your wallet.

832   This combination of numbers indicates that an ambition or passion from long ago will be fulfilled in the coming month.

833   This combination of numbers indicates that danger looms over you in the coming month, especially on even-numbered dates.

834   This combination of numbers indicates that a problem from long ago will be solved.

835   This combination of numbers indicates that a successful financial investment will change your life for the better.

836   This combination of numbers is important for a childless woman... During the coming year, you will have a child!

837   This combination of numbers indicates that memories you wished to forget will emerge and complicate your life.

838   This combination of numbers indicates that a plan you devised will collapse totally, and the heavy damages incurred will increase relentlessly.

839   This combination of numbers indicates that there is a danger involving water. Be careful!

840   This combination of numbers indicates that there is a disaster concerning stairs or a ladder looming over you or someone close to you.

841   This combination of numbers indicates that anything to do with the numbers 3 or 7 will bring you bad luck in the coming month.

842   This combination of numbers indicates that profligate spending will erode your financial basis.

843   This combination of numbers indicates that an invitation to some ordinary function will provide you with an opportunity for a dazzling future.

844   This combination of numbers advises you not to let a passing mood cloud your love life.

845   This combination of numbers indicates that you are on a dangerous track, both for your health and for your property.

846   This combination of numbers advises you to operate very energetically and with faith, and within a short time, you will accomplish your objective.

847   This combination of numbers indicates that this year, too, you can expect difficulties, but at the end of the year, your situation will improve.

848   This combination of numbers warns you not to make any decision in the coming week because substantial loss and damage are in the offing.

849   This combination of numbers indicates that a seemingly insignificant proposal can turn out to be a golden opportunity.

850   This combination of numbers indicates that there will be a change in place of work or place of residence in the coming year.

851   This combination of numbers indicates that there will be a real disappointment in matters of the heart.

852   This combination of numbers indicates that the influence of a member of the opposite sex will be beneficial to you in the near future.

853   This combination of numbers indicates that you can expect problems caused by the actions of younger members of your family.

854   This combination of numbers indicates a substantial lack of confidence in everything you do.

855   This combination of numbers warns you not to discount a warning that you received by chance, because a great deal of danger lies in wait for you.

856   This combination of numbers indicates that a real threat exists for people you love. Only you can protect them.

857   This combination of numbers indicates that you tend to play with fire, and this is not a very wise thing to do.

858   This combination of numbers indicates that you can expect pleasant surprises in the near future.

859   This combination of numbers indicates that news or an announcement from abroad will change your future for the better.

860   This combination of numbers indicates that you will soon have to face a strong and influential opponent.

861   This combination of numbers indicates that a trip abroad in the coming year is dangerous both for you and for those accompanying you.

862   This combination of numbers indicates that there is a danger of a serious illness with grave long-term consequences.

863   This combination of numbers indicates that you will be successful if you operate according to the destiny that was determined the moment you were born.

864   This combination of numbers for a man means that he has realized his vocation. For a woman, it is a warning of disappointment in love.

865   This combination of numbers indicates that you have to break an old tie that is holding you back in order to advance courageously.

866   This combination of numbers says that you will take courageous steps in order to realize your ambitions.

867   This combination of numbers encourages the purchase of land and property because the future holds a great deal of wealth in store for you.

868   This combination of numbers foretells success in everything to do with music and the theatrical arts.

869   This combination of numbers indicates that an improvement can be expected in the near future in everything to do with money and property.

870   This combination of numbers advises you to think ten times before investing your money.

871   This combination of numbers indicates that the coming years will be good and happy in comparison to recent years.

872   This combination of numbers says that you must not give other people control of your affairs because they will betray you.

873   This combination of numbers says that a difficult period is in the offing, and you will have to get through this difficult trial.

874   This combination of numbers says that you must not take pointless risks in the coming week since you are liable to get hurt.

875   This combination of numbers advises you to beware of a disease that starts with a cold and a fever.

876   This combination of numbers indicates that a business proposal that looks tempting will turn out to be fraudulent.

877   This combination of numbers augurs well for people belonging to earth signs.

878   This combination of numbers advises you to guard yourself against a new acquaintance, who is scheming to hurt you.

879   This combination of numbers is a warning that you are not looking after your health sufficiently.

880   This combination of numbers indicates that your suspicion of a close friend is unfounded, and will harm your relationship.

881   This combination of numbers is bad news for anyone who is connected with water or the sea.

882   This combination of numbers indicates that in the coming month, Saturdays and Sundays are bad days for you.

883   This combination of numbers indicates that important information is on its way to you, and you must study this information very seriously.

884   This combination of numbers indicates that you will have a new opportunity, and you must take full advantage of it.

885   This combination of numbers indicates that you must not support a plan with which you are not in complete agreement.

886   This combination of numbers indicates that a plan in which you invested a great deal of time will fail and cause you substantial loss.

887   This combination of numbers indicates that you must not gamble or risk an investment that relies on luck.

888   This combination of numbers indicates that you have got onto a dead-end street in which stupidity far outweighs wisdom.

889   This combination of numbers is a warning against error or failure in the management of your financial affairs.

890   This combination of numbers advises you to refrain from doing business with relatives because you are liable to suffer serious damage.

891   This combination of numbers indicates that honor and fame will be your lot if you fulfill all your obligations.

892   This combination of numbers indicates that a person who wishes you ill is watching every step you take.

893   This combination of numbers indicates that someone is out to get you, but the sign says that you will not be harmed.

894   This combination of numbers indicates that in the near future, there will not be any improvement in your situation.

895   This combination of numbers is a warning against physical injury or a serious disease.

896   This combination of numbers indicates that despite disappointments and difficulties, you will realize your aspirations this year.

897   This combination of numbers indicates that you can expect good health in the coming year, and even more important... true love.

898   This combination of numbers indicates that there will be an essential change in your life – probably in your occupation.

899   This combination of numbers indicates that great devotion and effort will be properly rewarded in the coming year.

900   This combination of numbers indicates that suspicions and intrigues in love will darken your life.

901   This combination of numbers indicates that many opportunities present themselves... but unfortunately you do not take advantage of them!

902   This combination of numbers is bad news for anyone involved in agriculture.

903   This combination of numbers says that you must not make any decisions about important things concerning money and property this week.

904   This combination of numbers indicates that a link to the religious realm will affect your life this week.

905   This combination of numbers indicates that a person whom you hardly know will exert a great influence on your life.

906   This combination of numbers is a warning against a serious illness or attack.

907   This combination of numbers indicates that difficulties in love are in the offing, even though everything seems to be fine on the surface.

908   This combination of numbers indicates that legal problems will come to an end in the coming year.

909   This combination of numbers advises you to plan your future carefully, since many obstacles lie ahead.

910   This combination of numbers indicates that marriage will be a blessing to you in the coming year.

911   This combination of numbers indicates that a long journey is in the offing. Its conclusion is unknown.

912   This combination of numbers indicates that the even months in the coming year are disastrous for you.

913   This combination of numbers is a grave warning about a serious accident.

914   This combination of numbers indicates that there will be a crisis in a love affair.

915   This combination of numbers indicates that you can expect a great deal of money in the future, but it won't reach you without a huge effort on your part.

916   This combination of numbers indicates that a domestic accident is in the offing in the coming month.

917   This combination of numbers foretells a separation – even by death – from someone who is very close to you.

918   This combination of numbers is a warning about an accident involving a vehicle.

919   This combination of numbers says that you must not invest in real estate this year because you are not thinking logically.

920   This combination of numbers indicates that you are vexed by opposing influences that distort your judgment.

921   This combination of numbers indicates that someone who was far from you until now will find a way to get close to you.

922   This combination of numbers advises you to face an approaching hardship with courage and boldness.

923   This combination of numbers foretells a change in place of residence – possibly even a move to another country.

924   This combination of numbers indicates that wealth and happiness will grow out of the relationship with one's mate.

925   This combination of numbers indicates that you can expect to work hard in the coming year.

926   This combination of numbers advises you to beware of a stranger who will hurt you unwittingly...

927   This combination of numbers is a warning of betrayal involving people close to you.

928   This combination of numbers indicates that you can expect joy and happiness as a result of the support of your friends.

929   This combination of numbers is a warning against adventures and risks, especially anything to do with the sea and mountain-climbing.

930   This combination of numbers indicates that in the coming year, you will pay dearly for a mistake you made a long time ago.

931   This combination of numbers advises you to pay attention to the signs of destiny! They are of great significance to you this month.

932   This combination of numbers indicates that a long journey will change your status and improve your financial situation.

933   This combination of numbers indicates that the influence of the opposite sex will be felt in the coming year.

934   This combination of numbers indicates that past difficulties will come back to torment you in the near future.

935   This combination of numbers indicates that you can expect a crisis in the business or professional realm. You will overcome it in the year ahead.

936   This combination of numbers advises you to be careful during your vacation because you are liable to get hurt.

937   This combination of numbers is bad news for anyone involved in gambling and... sport.

938   This combination of numbers indicates that you must not make hasty decisions. Exercise your discretion over and over again.

939   This combination of numbers indicates that a connection with a person with a bad reputation will damage your status.

940   This combination of numbers advises you to guard your money well because you will need it urgently in the near future.

941   This combination of numbers advises you to take advantage of the opportunity you have been offered – it won't happen twice.

942   This combination of numbers indicates that plans and ambitions will soon be realized, mainly thanks to your mate and friends.

943   This combination of numbers says that you must not ignore changes in your health, as these are liable to indicate a serious disease.

944   This combination of numbers advises you to be careful of financial obligations that you will not be able to fulfill.

945   This combination of numbers tells you not to expect help from a person whom you trust now in times of trouble.

946   This combination of numbers indicates that the future looks unclear, and it will be difficult rather than easy.

947   This combination of numbers indicates that marital problems are in the offing as a result of betrayals and infidelities.

948   This combination of numbers says that you must not give in to an urge or whim, since this will lead you down a bad path.

949   This combination of numbers indicates that you can expect advancement at work or an increase in status as a result of your hard work.

950   This combination of numbers indicates that anyone who is involved in writing or the creative arts will be successful.

951   This combination of numbers indicates that a crisis that will occur in the near future will be resolved in the long run.

952   This combination of numbers advises you to refrain from unnecessary expenditure because your resources are dwindling.

953   This combination of numbers indicates that if you are suffering from a health problem, you will be cured in the coming year.

954   This combination of numbers indicates that the direction of your life at present is leading you to perdition!

955   This combination of numbers indicates that suspecting and envying others will cause you to fail in life.

956   This combination of numbers indicates that a close friend is betraying you and mocking you behind your back.

957   This combination of numbers indicates that a member of the opposite sex will have a great influence on your life.

958   This combination of numbers indicates that an opportunity that seemed attractive and tempting will turn out to be a real trap!

959   This combination of numbers hardly has any significance... but it emphasizes the importance of the last dream you dreamed.

960   This combination of numbers indicates that new acquaintances will influence your life in the future.

961   This combination of numbers indicates that you can expect failure and troubles in the coming year.

962   This combination of numbers says that you must avail yourself of your friends and their advice in order to avoid getting embroiled in a serious complication.

963   This combination of numbers indicates that an aspiration from long ago will be realized in a surprising manner.

964   This combination of numbers indicates that this year, all lovers will learn that love is no bed of roses!

965　　This combination of numbers indicates that your luck will improve this year, but only in the financial realm.

966　　This combination of numbers indicates that a new acquaintance will undermine your existing way of life.

967　　This combination of numbers indicates that you can expect success in the social and economic realms alongside personal problems.

968　　This combination of numbers indicates that a friend who is virtually a member of your household will betray you.

969　　This combination of numbers indicates that a plan in which you invested a great deal of time will collapse before you can implement it.

970　　This combination of numbers indicates that there could be an unexpected windfall from a lottery or from a good investment.

971　　This combination of numbers indicates that a serious occurrence will strengthen existing love.

972　　This combination of numbers tells you to stop insisting on a plan that you don't believe in wholeheartedly.

973　　This combination of numbers indicates that an investment in the coming month will turn out to yield good returns.

974　　This combination of numbers indicates that too much self-confidence is liable to harm your economic status.

975　　This combination of numbers indicates that despite difficulties and hardships, you can attain success by means of hard work and sticking to the plans.

976　　This combination of numbers indicates that help will come to you from a faraway relative whose existence you were hardly aware of.

977   This combination of numbers indicates that your efforts will bear fruit, but this fruit will be a bad bargain.

978   This combination of numbers foretells danger from food that comes from the sea.

979   This combination of numbers advises you to guard yourself against "bureaucratic" damage because it is liable to be very painful.

980   This combination of numbers will strengthen your hand – your ambitions will be realized in the near future.

981   This combination of numbers indicates that the death of someone close to you will have a tremendous effect on your life.

982   This combination of numbers indicates that dark clouds will be dispersed by the wind. Look ahead and follow the path you choose.

983   This combination of numbers indicates that a separation or a death in the family is in the offing, involving one of your relatives.

984   This combination of numbers indicates that there will be a change of luck in the coming year, for better or for worse – who knows?

985   This combination of numbers indicates that someone is holding you back, but you will overcome them by force.

986   This combination of numbers advises you to continue along your path with caution, since you are approaching a dangerous fork in it.

987   This combination of numbers indicates that in the coming year, you will become very close to someone you love.

988   This combination of numbers indicates that you can expect a long journey... but it would be preferable for you to stay at home.

989   This combination of numbers indicates that there is an unpleasant surprise in store for you within the walls of your home.

990   This combination of numbers indicates that good luck awaits you far away, but you have to leave your home and go out and get it!

991   This combination of numbers indicates that the wheel of fortune is spinning in your favor. Take the opportunity when it presents itself.

992   This combination of numbers indicates that disappointments and failures in your business and personal life are in the offing.

993   This combination of numbers tells you not to gamble in the coming month, since you will be out of luck.

994   This combination of numbers indicates that news from an unknown factor is likely to change your life.

995   This combination of numbers advises you to operate according to your impulses or intuition, otherwise you will miss the correct path.

996   This combination of numbers indicates that instead of worrying about status and honor, you should be worrying about material matters.

997   This combination of numbers indicates that you must cultivate your spiritual life, even if this comes at the expense of your material life.

998   This combination of numbers indicates an injustice you must correct in order to reach your true goal.

999   This combination of numbers tells you not to trust a stranger, because a trap for the gullible awaits you.

A summary of predictions (sample page)

Day 1
Essence of the prediction _____
Did it come true? _____

Day 2
Essence of the prediction _____
Did it come true? _____

Day 3
Essence of the prediction _____
Did it come true? _____

Day 4
Essence of the prediction _____
Did it come true? _____

Day 5
Essence of the prediction _____
Did it come true? _____

Day 6
Essence of the prediction _____
Did it come true? _____

Day 7
Essence of the prediction _____
Did it come true? _____

The Winning Number!

Numerological Compatibility

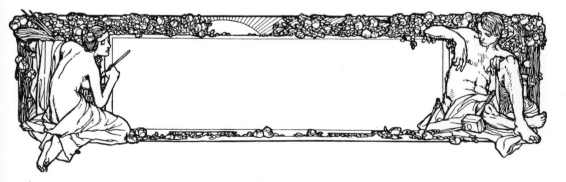

Boy meets girl, girl meets boy...

How compatible are they?

This part of the book examines the compatibility between women's personal numbers and men's personal numbers. This compatibility will enable you to discover and examine an additional aspect of your relationship with your mate.

In this part of the book, the characteristics of people's personal numbers focus on the sexual realm. The personal number is calculated according to the person's first name, with each letter being translated into its numerical value, adding them up, and then reducing the sum until a single digit, from 1 to 9, is obtained.

People whose personal number is 1

It's enough to look at the shape of a number 1 to know that love and sex must be consummated. For them, love that is not consummated is not perfect. (You must remember that there is no difference between men and women in this.) Consummating sex and love requires, to some extent, penetration into the personal realm of another person, because nothing can be consummated when number 1 is alone.

This means that logic, reason, and social norms dictate number 1's sexuality. The emotional consideration is relegated to second place in the relationship. In other words, if we want to characterize number 1 from the point of view of sexuality, we can go to the ordinary and common aspects of the society in which he lives, according to both the lifestyle and the "schedule" in which everything happens.

Number 1 people are very physical in their love, and must go through the whole routine in order to feel that "they're OK." And this does not only concern the matter of penetration, which is characterized as a central factor in number 1 people.

Their love is sensual, and it is difficult to find number 1 people whose love is solely "platonic." At a young age, love is expressed through curiosity and an attempt to consummate sexuality, but after they have settled down somewhat, there is a decrease in their sexuality. The fact that for number 1 people, love and sexuality are linked to physical consummation hits them like a boomerang at a later age, because "if it isn't consummated... it isn't love!"

People whose personal number is 2

Many numerologists make the mistake of seeing number 2's sexuality as the continuation of number 1's sexuality – the first is active and the second is passive, the first bursts in and the second receives... Those numerologists are well advised to consult their textbooks again, because they are wrong, and they mislead many people in this delicate realm of love and sexuality.

In fact, the sexuality of number 2's should be viewed as if number 2 were composed of two number 1's standing back to back. What does this mean? Number 2's have a substantial sexual appetite, meaning an appetite for variety, change, and innovation rather than an appetite for more and more helpings of the same familiar dish.

The sexuality of people whose personal number is 2 is a "given," but they are also aware of the fact that love and sexual relationships are created by the interaction between the members of the couple. The more they swap and vary partners, the more aspects of their sexuality they discover.

For this reason, they are constantly on the lookout for "new" partners, preferably also different ones. The image of two number 1's "back-to-back" implies that number 2's are always seeking opportunities in the realm of love and sex, and this is why they have the reputation of being Don Juans. On the other hand, the variety in their relationships does not guarantee especially good sexuality, and in the realm of love, it is more of a liability than an asset. Number 2's love does not derive from the depths of emotion, either; it is based mainly on impulses expressed by the logic that realizing impulses is a way of life for them.

People whose personal number is 3

Great! Number 3's bring emotion into the picture. Don't make light of this – number 3's display intense sexuality and loyal love that endures for a long time, and is not dependent on the thing itself.

Many people see number 3's as the first to consummate the love between the members of a couple, and operate according to the principle of "it takes two to tango." To a great extent, there is numerological truth in this, originating from the general properties of number 3.

Number 3 is an indication of properties of love and sexuality that are expressed very intensely, with great passion, and at the same time remain stable for a long time. Although this is not a guarantee for the "quality" of the relationship, in most cases the amount of intensity is sufficient in itself. Thus, number 3's are considered to have good and – more important – stable sexuality and love.

There is a lot of importance to the fact that number 3's love with "emotion" – emotion being the glue that unites and safeguards love for a long time. For example, these people do not experience a decrease in their physical capacity for love in the second half of their lives.

There is no doubt that, as a "serious" partner, number 3 has a certain advantage over numbers 1 and 2. However, before choosing, you should check out the other numbers.

People whose personal number is 4

Number 4 people are square – everyone knows that. However, this definition by itself is inadequate in the realm of sexuality and love. In fact, this definition even does these people an injustice.

The principal and leading property of number 4's is "slowness and thoroughness." They don't rush, they aren't tempted to hurry (and they do not let go easily). The development of their love and sexuality is slow, and is based on the balance between emotions and physicality, between passion and love. Moreover, in order to reach the stage of a relationship, they must be convinced, both logically and emotionally, that they are doing the right thing.

In other words, the stage of checking and examining, touching and feeling, is the longest and most important one in number 4's sexuality, and the slowness in the development of the relationship often causes the potential partner to "snap." However, the moment the relationship has been established, all the components have been examined, and all the conclusions drawn, number 4's love reaches its maximal expression.

At this stage, number 4's reveal intense, fundamental, and ongoing sexuality, and their love is balanced, true, and enduring. There is no doubt that after the tentative stage, number 4's, despite their "squareness," reveal a stable and beautiful aspect of love and sexuality.

People whose personal number is 5

In the realm of love and sexuality, number 5's are in the middle of the road; they reveal all the positive properties – and all the negative ones – in love and sex. Since this is the case, they manifest a nervous, jumpy, and unpredictable attitude toward this realm.

Number 5's sexuality is not extraordinarily good, but their enthusiasm and the way they stick to their objective make up for it. Many people say that number 5's are people who have "magnets in the seat of their pants." They operate according to the factor next to them, to which they are attracted, or which they attract. When the object changes, the magnet changes its course.

Number 5's are the lovers about whom countless books have been written... and they are the same jealous and cheating lovers whose stories are splashed all over the crime pages of the newspapers. They are people who can captivate – or repel!

Number 5's main problem is getting the relationship of sexuality and love past the stage of the fling. This is a real problem. Their lives are full of crises and ups and downs in this important area of life.

Number 5's are a real gamble, as far as numerologists are concerned – their behavior is unpredictable, and because of this, the numerologist has a hard time characterizing what is in store for them. But it is important to remember that love and sexuality are, in fact, this person's main "trigger" or activator in the emotional realm.

People whose personal number is 6

As we know, number 6's are influenced by the planet Venus, and most numerologists conclude from this that love, for which Venus is responsible, is the central energy that nourishes people with this personal number. (Some numerologists go further and determine that the requisite match for number 6 is number 9, who is dominated by the energy of Mars. Together, we get a marvelously compatible combination of 69!)

Modern numerology tries to examine the people with a particular personal number without reference to the planetary influence in order to produce profound and thorough explanations, together with instructions for "action." For this reason, they examine the number 6 through the eyes of a Star of David.

The accepted shape of a Star of David is two superimposed triangles – one pointing downward and one pointing upward. The numerologist sees the first one as the triangle of sexuality, and the second one as the triangle of love. The first and main problem of number 6 people is to keep the two triangles in perfect balance – otherwise the Star of David will disintegrate into meaningless components!

Thus, number 6's work at maintaining the balance of love and sexuality, and their whole lives – both for themselves and for their relationship – is devoted to this task. Don't disparage this; there are very few people for whom this balance is natural and does not require a constant major effort.

On the practical level, number 6's seek to balance love and sexuality, and we don't know at which level the two components become balanced. Number 6's do not search for the level – but rather the balance.

People whose personal number is 7

Number 7's mainly reveal their vulnerability to the energy of love and sex. This means that the person wants "to be" in love, wants to "make the most of" sexuality, and wants to "radiate" love. In other words, the impression is no less important than the actual thing!

Quite naturally, number 7's expose this aspect of their lives mainly when there is a breakdown or a crisis in the energy of love and sexuality. Have you ever tried being in a love nest with a number 7 who has lost his strength? He reacts as if he has been stripped stark naked in the town square, and all his acquaintances are throwing rotten eggs at him.

This is the reason that number 7's sensitivity, not to mention vulnerability, comes to the fore mainly during crises, or when number 7's are "between loves." This causes them to live their love and sex lives "on the razor's edge," investing a great deal of energy and tension in this realm. This is the reason why many of them choose "theory" instead of "practice" – that is, they prefer the spirituality of love to its physical and "material" consummation.

People whose personal number is 8

Number 8's can claim – rightfully – that numerologists have done them an injustice, mainly because they've given them the reputation of coldness... and the distance from this point to describing them as "walking refrigerators" is short.

This is not the case. First of all, number 8's are people with good, strong sexuality – often quite impressive. Except that, unfortunately for them, they remind us of the joke about bald men: In theory, they are the most virile of the male sex... but in practice, they don't have the chance to prove it!

It is the same with number 8's. Their strong sexuality is often wasted because they do everything slowly, cool-headedly, after testing, examining, and investigating. After they have done all of this, another door is slammed in their face!

It is difficult for number 8's to understand that the realm of love and sex is one where more is hidden than is shown. They operate according to a formula they have prepared in advance, and they will never add salt to the soup before adding pepper...

It is important for us to differentiate between number 8's feeling out the road and his conquering the objective, since there is a tremendous difference between these two stages in his life. It is important that number 8's know how to differentiate between the end and the means they employ to achieve it – for their own good.

People whose personal number is 9

Number 9's constitute a problem for numerologists who rely on astrology. They realize the energy of number 1, balance number 6, and are ruled by the masculine planet Mars! Numerologists are well aware of this, but when they set out to examine the properties of a number 9 in the realm of love and sexuality, they discover that the reality is different than the theory of the stars.

Numerology must view number 9's sexuality and love in a different way. On the one hand, they are intensely sexual, which derives from their being the product of 3 times 3; on the other hand, they are very loyal, which derives from their being the recurring number of the circle of the primary numerological numbers.

So, despite the fact that number 9's lack "the emotion of love," the combination of sexuality and fidelity makes up for the lack of emotion in their character. They are considerate of their mates, view their mates' needs as their own, and pay attention to every "complaint" or squeak in their relations. If we view number 9's in this light, we will better understand their route along the paths of love and sexuality.

The matching is performed according to women's personal numbers (1 to 9). Men's numbers appear under all the women's headings, in consecutive order.

The number 1 woman

A number 1 woman with a number 1 man

The combination of a number 1 woman with a number 1 man is excellent.

This is a special number, primary and creative, and so it involves an ambitious woman who will do everything in her power to accomplish her objectives. She is independent and determined, and aspires to realize her aims together with a loving mate.

A number 1 man's properties are very similar to hers. He will never be dragged along after her, but will walk along a common path where they are equals. This is a man who is aware of himself and of his strength and power, so the match between them is perfect!

This is not a relationship of controller and controlled, or puller and pulled. It is a relationship of mutual giving and taking that fertilizes each other. Decisions are made together, without a feeling of frustration or deprivation.

All this, of course, only exists if there is cooperation between the two. If there isn't, the endless power of each of them is liable to cause them to pull in different directions, and then not only will they not achieve harmony – the diametric opposite will occur.

If they learn to cooperate, nothing will stand in their way. Two such "bulldozers" in harmonious cooperation constitute a winning team in anyone's book.

The woman is the one who leads the relationship, since the list has been made according to the woman's personal number. She has the right to choose, and, in fact, everything depends on her.

If she learns to harness the man to her objectives, the couple's success is guaranteed, in parallel with safeguarding their relationship. However, if the woman tries to be too aggressive and exploits her positive characteristics to subdue all the abilities of the man who is with her, so that she can prove that she is no less equal than he is, the relationship won't stand a chance; it will soon break up and lose its uniqueness.

The rating on the numerological scale of love: 8

A number 1 woman with a number 2 man

The combination of a number 1 woman with a number 2 man is can be extreme - either very good or very bad.

Number 2 is a female, feminine number.

It is hard to believe that an ambitious, aggressive woman who knows what she wants out of life, who is slightly "masculine" as a number 1 is, will want to enter a relationship with a man who has feminine properties. On the one hand, she will aspire to find the properties that complement her in the man, but on the other, she may want a man whose properties are even more masculine and aggressive than hers are.

A number 2 man will be passive, inclined to let his wife lead, and willing to follow in her footsteps.

The big advantage in such a relationship is that the number 1 woman will not consider the number 2 man a partner with whom she has to compete. On the contrary: he will be willing to give her a hand in her race toward success. He will support her all the way. He will be prepared to assume the burden of the home, the children, and so on. He will be able to give her her due, and be proud of and happy about her success.

If this is the case, both partners will learn to manifest the strong sides of their personalities, and to complement each other, and then it can be a marvelous relationship.

If, on the other hand, the man feels deprived, and feels that his talents are not coming to the fore because his wife fills up their entire conjugal space, the relationship will be fraught with danger, and liable to break up.

The rating on the numerological scale of love: 6+

A number 1 woman with a number 3 man

A number 3 man unites both the properties of number 1 and those of number 2 in his personal number. That is – he actually creates perfection.

Having said that, the dominance of the number 1 woman is so great that in spite of the positive and almost perfect characteristics of the man who is with her, she is still liable to make him feel that he is always in a position of inferiority.

If the number 1 woman knows how to fit the number 3 man into her life and create a relationship of equal partnership, together they will make up the combination of 4, and then it will be a long-lasting relationship.

If there is a lack of equality in the relationship, it is difficult to say that their life together will be a rose garden.

The number 1 woman, because of her dominant character, is liable to relate to the number 3 man who is with her as if he is a plaything rather than a life partner and her mate to all extents and purposes.

The rating on the numerological scale of love: 6

A number 1 woman with a number 4 man

The number 4 man likes to see himself fixed up and settled; he is a person whose life moves along a fixed and known route. He likes to know that he has a firm economic basis, and the attendant peace of mind is important to him.

In contrast, the number 1 woman cannot rest on her laurels. She is constantly aspiring to accomplish new aims, realize far-off goals, and conquer as many objectives as possible.

On the surface, it seems as if these two can't get on. But because the number 4 includes number 1, the two will discover, after their first meeting, that they complement each other amazingly well.

The man guarantees his mate a safe, emotional, stable, and faithful relationship. He contributes to her peace of mind and does his bit by being responsible for the material side of life and freeing her of worries and of risk-taking. He is calculating and responsible.

The woman breaks frameworks and breaches borders. She can allow herself this luxury when she knows there is someone standing behind her and supporting her totally, because such is the number 4 man.

This is a good, trusting, solid, strong relationship, and it is very difficult to undermine its foundations. When it is accompanied by powerful love, it can reach perfection.

The rating on the numerological scale of love: 9-

A number 1 woman with a number 5 man

The number 5 man is generally very preoccupied with himself and with developing his personality, and likes to concentrate on his pleasures and on the realization of his dreams.

The number 1 woman likes to complement the man's characteristics. It doesn't look like she can adapt to a relationship with a number 5 man who is constantly preoccupied with himself.

Although he can be a marvelous lover because of those very properties, in due course she will need a relationship with a man who can give her much more than that. Not recommended.

The rating on the numerological scale of love: 5-

A number 1 woman with a number 6 man

A number 1 woman with a number 6 man can be an interesting combination, because together they make up the sum of 7... Having said that, there is greater risk than gain.

A number 6 man is seeking comfort. He enjoys being in a pampering environment in which he does not have to make an effort or go to too much trouble. It won't bother him in the least to sit at home and let his wife support him, or to earn less than she does, as long as he is set up financially and has an easy life.

The danger lies in number 1 woman's dominance of a man like this. Because of his character, she is liable to force a way of life or certain behavior patterns on him that suit her needs, but not his.

Ultimately, this can lead to an explosion. The woman is the one who has the power to determine the nature of the relationship. It is entirely in her control.

The rating on the numerological scale of love: 7+

A number 1 woman with a number 7 man

The number 1 woman is much more practical than the number 7 man. He likes to debate and philosophize, while she wants action, and even daring deeds.

They aren't on the same wavelength, and in fact are operating on two different planes. He operates on the conceptual plane. She operates on the practical plane. It is difficult to imagine a full and happy family life with such a combination.

Indeed, it would seem that with the woman being responsible for the practical side, and living in a totally physical and earthy world, and her mate floating in the philosophical plane, this would be a perfect relationship. However, we are often witnesses to the fact that such a relationship cannot stand the test of reality.

The rating on the numerological scale of love: 5

A number 1 woman with a number 8 man

The number 1 woman can find the number 8 man to be an ideal partner in everything concerning friendship and companionship; he may even be a great business partner. All this is true as long as there is no question of love, sex, or marriage.

The number 8 man may be the perfect combination for her characteristics. But when the relationship becomes personal, the two of them are liable to run into serious problems: the number 8 man is very stubborn. He is not a compromising type, and it will be very difficult for him to accept an ambitious, career-oriented woman like the number 1 type. He will always prefer a submissive woman who sits at home and is available for him at all times.

The rating on the numerological scale of love: 6

A number 1 woman with a number 9 man

A number 9 man is blessed with a marvelous property: he can adapt himself to the properties of (almost) any woman, especially in the personal realm.

He always knows what her vulnerable points and weaknesses are, where her strengths lie, what she is feeling, if she is happy, satisfied, disappointed, and what her state of mind is. He is blessed with the ability to sense when his wife needs reinforcement, when she doesn't, and so on.

The combination of 1 and 9 is 10, which is $1 + 0 = 1$. That is, the woman doesn't lose anything, and returns to a stronger starting point because of the man beside her.

As long as people around do not know the nature of their relationship, and the number 9 man's self-respect is not undermined because the woman is leading the relationship and he must adapt himself to her, and not the opposite – the relationship will endure for a long time.

The rating on the numerological scale of love: 9+

The number 2 woman

A number 2 woman with a number 1 man

This is a combination of a woman with the most characteristic feminine number and a man with the most characteristic masculine number. The combination of both of them is 3, a number that indicates development and growth.

The number 2 woman complements the properties of the number 1 man, and vice versa. The two serve as each other's helpmeets. This is an almost ideal situation between the members of a couple, because they will never hold a grudge against each other, and there won't be any residual bitterness resulting from one's achievements at the expense of the other.

This kind of relationship will not be truly perfect if the woman is too "feminine." If she pampers herself too much, and devotes more attention to herself than to her husband – even if she does it for him, to please him – there may be glitches in their relationship.

The number 2 woman loves to be "all woman." She is the classic *femme fatale*. When her partner accepts these characteristics, encourages her desire to emphasize them and understands her inability to behave otherwise, a combination like this, which enables the woman to realize her femininity and make the most of her characteristics, will be ideal for both parties.

The rating on the numerological scale of love: 9

A number 2 woman with a number 2 man

This is a combination of two people who are very similar – almost identical – in all their properties. They don't need to talk to each other, because they understand each other via body language and looks only. They understand each other, and each one helps with the development of the other by recognizing his/her needs and comprehending his/her emotions and demands.

Since the number 2 man is liable to have slightly "feminine" properties, such as a lack of independence, assertiveness, or initiative, a situation could arise in which although he very much wants to help the woman beside him, his ability to do so is limited.

The danger in such a relationship is that the woman will look for what she lacks outside of their conjugal bond. Her partner will not only understand her deeds, but will blame himself for the situation.

Another danger that is liable to be inherent in such a relationship is that over the course of time, the man will not be able to take upon himself totally the role of the one who frequently complements the woman's properties, and this may lead to problems.

Having said that, the combination of 2 + 2 is 4, which itself attests to a stable, enduring relationship, provided that each member of the couple agrees to assume his/her role in the relationship without reservations.

The rating on the numerological scale of love: 7+

A number 2 woman with a number 3 man

The combination of a number 2 woman with a number 3 man makes 5, which is generally an individual personal number that does not characterize couples. Having said that, it indicates a relationship on a high personal level.

Both members of the couple are self-aware and know what they want. The number 3 man likes the woman beside him to be submissive, obedient, loving, and pampering. Indeed, the number 2 woman could easily fill those requirements if the suitable man were only at her side. It seems that this is not the case with a number 3 man, however. He sees women in a stereotypical way: for him, a woman is a woman, and from his point of view, there is no great difference in basic characteristics between one woman and the next.

The number 2 woman, who is well aware of the difference between her and other women, will not accept this attitude – so that even if they seem to be perfect together, they are in fact far from being the ideal couple.

The rating on the numerological scale of love: 6+

A number 2 woman with a number 4 man

The number 4 man sees the world from a rational point of view. He is very tidy and organized, a bit "square," and finds it difficult to accept changes and be spontaneous. Conversely, the number 2 woman loves to blur the borders between her and the world around her, and be part of it.

The relationship between them will usually not be based on warm, deep feelings, or on passion and raging emotions. There will be something utilitarian about it that stems from a logical calculation. The number 2 woman brings her creativity, her enthusiasm, and her intuitive ability to the relationship, while the number 4 man contributes his properties of stability and practicality.

We can say that a relationship like this, in the right dosage, will be very stable for years, as long as they both pull their weight in their home and in the family life they build together.

The rating on the numerological scale of love: 7

A number 2 woman with a number 5 man

The number 5 man is a bit egoistic. He recognizes his value, and likes to look at himself (and admire what he sees). The properties that characterize him are too similar to those of the number 2 woman. And she needs a man who will look at her, not at himself.

This relationship is practically doomed from the outset. In order for it to survive, the number 2 woman must negate herself in favor of the man who is with her, and become the submissive and dominated woman who does not express her own needs, but rather only takes the needs of her partner into consideration.

And this won't happen to a number 2 woman! She will never forego her acknowledgment of her femininity and sexuality.

The rating on the numerological scale of love: 4+

A number 2 woman with a number 6 man

The number 6 man complements the properties of the number 2 woman. He is spontaneous and creative, but does not allow himself to overdo these properties.

The number 2 woman ensures that she provides him with the confidence to fulfill his desire to progress and develop. They are very supportive of each other, without detracting from each other's properties.

This relationship will be particularly successful if the couple don't demand too much of life, because there is something of an "energy depletion" in their relationship. There is no one to pull them forward toward development and daring, and sometimes they remain stuck in a groove.

The rating on the numerological scale of love: 8

A number 2 woman with a number 7 man

The number 7 man is blessed with the ability to adapt himself to almost any woman. He knows his trade well, and knows how to charm women, even if he sometimes appears soft, obsequious, and snake-like.

The number 7 man can be the love of the number 2 woman's life, but not for long, it seems. This is a relationship that is doomed to break up. Even if the number 2 woman does everything in her power to help and support the number 7 man along his path in life, she will repeatedly encounter difficulties and cause him to face recurrent resounding failures against his will.

A number 7 man can, however, be a perfect lover for the feminine number 2 woman.

The rating on the numerological scale of love: 6-

A number 2 woman with a number 8 man

The number 8 man is blessed with wonderful properties: he is diligent, practical, stable, and the kind who can always be depended on. A man like this is every number 2 woman's fantasy.

The combination of the two will help the number 8 man find his masculinity at the side of the feminine number 2 woman.

This is a perfect relationship: the man feels that the woman with him is his helpmeet who helps him realize his desires and ambitions, while she is in seventh heaven because she found herself a match like this.

The rating on the numerological scale of love: 8+

A number 2 woman with a number 9 man

If there could be a perfect man for the number 2 woman, it would have to be the number 9 man. He has all the properties that help the number 2 woman make the most of her femininity, but, having said that, this does not prevent the number 9 man from fulfilling himself and safeguarding his character and personality.

This is the ideal model of a happy family, in which each member of the couple achieves the realization of his personality without detracting from the development of the other.

If the number 9 man has an Achilles heel, it is ironically weak masculinity, but his success in all other areas makes up for it, and does not jeopardize the happiness of the couple.

The rating on the numerological scale of love: 10-

The number 3 woman

A number 3 woman with a number 1 man

The essence of the number 3 woman's character is determined according to her relationship and combination with her partner, and according to the nature of the relations that develop between them.

In a number 3 woman, one can find both feminine and masculine characteristics. Therefore, sometimes a number 1 partner will complement her characteristics, and sometimes they will be part of their common characteristics, and perhaps also identity.

She is an impulsive, spontaneous woman who doesn't always determine her steps logically, but rather according to her emotions and feelings at the particular moment. This dominant property, which is considered by many to add a special touch to her relationship with her partner, is liable to constitute a source of problems and crises – particularly in a relationship with a number 1 man.

The number 1 man likes a peaceful and quiet life along a path that is more or less known in advance, without unnecessary "surprises."

Having said that, it is a relationship that is basically stable, because the combination of 3 + 1 = 4 creates a relationship of stability and power. The bond between the two will be one of ups and downs, of moments of supreme happiness contrasted with bitter disappointments, but it will last for a long time.

The rating on the numerological scale of love: 7

A number 3 woman with a number 2 man

The combination of the two, which makes 5, results in a personal number and not in that of a family unit. The number 3 woman tends to reinforce her feminine side. On the other hand, the properties of the number 2 man are in essence also properties that tend toward the feminine.

Therefore, if the number 3 woman is inclined to look for a partner with masculine properties, who will be her helpmeet, the relationship with a number 2 man will not be outstandingly successful. If she has a tendency toward passive femininity only, and this femininity is not her dominant characteristic, the chances of a successful relationship with a number 2 man are much greater.

Having said that, it must be remembered that the number 2 man is a very stable person, who likes an orderly and organized life. The number 3 woman's impulsiveness and spontaneity are liable to constitute a threat for him, so the chances of this type of relationship succeeding are small.

The rating on the numerological scale of love: 5+

A number 3 woman with a number 3 man

The properties of a number 3 man are almost identical to those of a number 3 woman. Both of them are prone to mood swings, both of them are ambitious, and both of them have both masculine and feminine properties.

Since the woman is the one who determines the type of relationship between them, she will never be bored with the number 3 man's properties. However, the rhythm and nature of their relations will be determined according to her moods, often (too often!) without allowing her partner to feel that he is part of them.

With preconditions like those, and despite the fact that the combination of 3 + 3 = 6 is a strong and capable number, a relationship that is based on the dominant desires of the woman, that is inherently capricious, and that depends on mood swings, will not be stable or interesting.

The rating on the numerological scale of love: 5

A number 3 woman with a number 4 man

In a combination like this – our number 3 woman with a number 4 man, who is by nature stable and organized – the two complement each other. The number 3 woman has all the properties that are missing in the number 4 man: spontaneity, developed feminine intuition, lightness, and unconventionality.

The number 4 man is generally attracted to a woman who is the diametric opposite of himself. He is grateful to her for showing him other facets of life and providing him with variety. This is an enduring and stable bond, and even if there are occasional misunderstandings or "blow-ups," the problems are usually solved to the satisfaction of both parties.

The rating on the numerological scale of love: 8-

A number 3 woman with a number 5 man

In a relationship like this, there is a measure of stability, because the combination of the number 3 woman with the number 5 man resembles the combination with the number 1 man. The difficulty in their relationship will mainly stem from the fact that the number 5 man is too involved with himself, his ambitions, and his desires, and it is difficult for him to share things with the number 3 woman, who likes things to be done her way.

From her point of view, she is the leader of the relationship, and her partner must adapt himself to her wishes and whims. This being the case, the relationship is almost impossible. Having said that, it occurs quite often, perhaps because of the fact that the combination of the two numbers – 8 – has a truly eternal life-span!

If a couple like this who have been living together for a long time can be found, it means that they entered this relationship with their eyes open from the start, and had no illusions about the dominant characteristics of the other member of the couple.

The rating on the numerological scale of love: 5

A number 3 woman with a number 6 man

The number 3 woman will find her properties – doubled – in a number 6 man.

From this point of view, the number 6 man knows exactly what to expect. The couple's common number – 9 – takes us back to 3 times 3. In other words, they realize the expectations that derive from the numerology of love of both of them together.

The cooperation between the two is good, and even more than that: they understand each other, are prepared to accept each other's quirks, enjoy an excellent sexual relationship, and are united in their desire to accomplish common objectives.

This relationship is good and fruitful, and brings out the good qualities of each of them.

The rating on the numerological scale of love: 9

A number 3 woman with a number 7 man

The relationship between a number 3 woman and an ambitious, spiritual, and talkative number 7 man tends toward the masculine side, mainly because of their combination, 3 + 7 = 10, that is 1.

Even if it looks like they are compatible at the beginning, over the course of time, after the relationship becomes more tightly knit, it looks like it is impossible. The man is liable to discover that the number 3 woman has more masculine properties than he has.

This is a relationship that lacks any common ground, and will not endure.

The rating on the numerological scale of love: 4+

A number 3 woman with a number 8 man

The number 8 man, who loves stability and order, and who has a great deal of patience, can be the perfect mate for the number 3 woman – if she were looking for a platonic relationship.

The number 8 man will enable the number 3 woman to realize her goals and aspirations in life, because he has the ability to serve as a stable leaning post for her and provide her with a strong, sturdy basis.

However, when it comes to personal relations, the number 8 man is not enough of a "man" for her. From her point of view, she leads him, instead of being led by him in the relationship, and she cannot stand that.

This is the reason why we often find in long-term relationships like this that the woman has taken a permanent lover on the side.

The rating on the numerological scale of love: 7-

A number 3 woman with a number 9 man

A relationship like this – between a number 3 woman and a number 9 man – solves nothing in the woman's life: 3 X 3 = 9, and 3 + 9 = 12, when 1 + 2 = 3 once again.

The number 9 man will be a nuisance in all areas of life: there will not be any cooperation between them, their aims will not be shared, nor will the path to self-realization. In contrast, in the personal realm, they are totally compatible.

It is important to remember that the woman is the leader in the relationship and determines its development. Therefore, the quality of the relationship, in fact, depends on her. She can maneuver her partner as she wishes. Either this will be a permanent relationship with a warm, loving home, or it will be a serious let-down.

The rating on the numerological scale of love: 7

The number 4 woman

A number 4 woman with a number 1 man

This is a stable, square woman who does not like change, and seeks security and peace of mind. In contrast, the number 1 man is a far more dynamic, creative, initiating type. Since the combination of the two numbers is 5, which is a personal number, it means that the properties of only one of the couple will be dominant in a relationship like this, and this is not the way to create a family unit or a long-term bond. If the number 4 woman dominates the relationship, the properties of the man with her will be "erased," and even if the number 1 man's properties prevail, the woman's stability will be undermined.

If this is a platonic relationship, for the sake of a common goal such as establishing a business, for example, it can be an ideal combination – she will provide the stability and the security, and he will provide the impetus, the initiative, and the daring.

The rating on the numerological scale of love: 5

A number 4 woman with a number 2 man

In a relationship like this, the woman finds her properties in the man opposite her, because he is in fact identical to her.

As we mentioned before, the number 4 woman is square and is blatantly feminine. But so is the number 2 man, who has a large measure of feminine properties. In such a relationship, the woman will be the leader, and the man will be led.

In the home of such a couple, "family squareness" will prevail. It will not produce any great initiatives. Nor will sparks fly from the bedroom. Both members of the couple prefer to work in modest but secure jobs that provide security in life – anything but taking unnecessary risks or embarking on superfluous adventures that will give them sleepless nights.

The rating on the numerological scale of love: 7-

A number 4 woman with a number 3 man

This kind of relationship is good and stable, and over the course of time will bring about the development of both members of the couple and make them fruitful.

The number 4 woman likes stability and security, and the number 3 man brings the very blatant and dominant masculine characteristics in his personality to the relationship. He is a man who is searching for security in the family unit, but at the same time, presses forward toward new challenges.

In such a relationship, properties of stability, security, and realism are at play alongside initiative, imagination, and creativity. It is fruitful for all kinds of relationships – business, interpersonal, and family – and it gives the couple the ability to cope with pressures and changes over the course of time.

The rating on the numerological scale of love: 8+

A number 4 woman with a number 4 man

The combination of 4 + 4 = 8 attests to "infinity."

This is a square couple whose relationship does not harm their personal bond. Both of them find happiness in this kind of relationship. The bond between them is excellent, and together they function as a pair that no one in the world can overcome.

If there is a flaw in such a relationship, it is the feminine basis, which is dominant in both of them. They both have the dominant characteristic of being considerate of other people, and of compromising with each other.

Sometimes, because they are too considerate, neither of them is willing to "take up the reins," so they are not decisive enough regarding their prospective path. However, this problem is a minor one in this relationship.

The rating on the numerological scale of love: 8+

A number 4 woman with a number 5 man

The combination of these two numbers is 9, which has many powers, and the ability to realize ambitions and create a long-term relationship.

Having said that, we must not forget that the typical number 5 man is very aware of himself and of his needs, and it can even be said that he is rather selfish.

The number 4 woman is looking for the united family unit, and she also wants to be the one who calls the tune in this family nest.

The relationship will go well provided that both of them have common goals and similar aims to unite them. If this is not the case, however, unbridgeable gaps are liable to appear in their relationship.

The number 5 man brings a new aspect of daring and innovation into his personal and sexual relationship with the number 4 woman – beyond her wildest dreams.

This can make the number 5 man feel that he is the man of the house, and will enable him to ignore the number 4 woman's desire to be the dominant one in the rest of the aspects of running the house.

The rating on the numerological scale of love: 8

A number 4 woman with a number 6 man

The relationship between these two is very good – possibly because of the combination of 4 + 6 = 10, which is 1.

A man with the number 6 tends to have feminine properties, and the number of the combination – 1 – balances this.

The number 6 man, like the number 4 woman, likes stability, reliability, and security, and seeks peace of mind. A relationship between a number 4 woman and a number 6 man is an "organized" one. There is a clear division of authority. Each one has his/her own space, and each one lets the other do his/her own thing, without disturbing him/her.

In this way, they each make the most of their abilities, talents, and outstanding qualities, and neither one feels frustrated because of the other. The fact that they both fulfill their potential leads to a warm and loving home, devoid of anger and frustration.

The rating on the numerological scale of love: 9+

A number 4 woman with a number 7 man

The combination of the two is 7 + 4 = 11; 1 + 1 = 2. This creates a strong couple with a great ability to make the most of its members' qualities.

The woman is "square" and the man has feminine properties in addition to masculine ones. He is a man of many talents, but he cannot get himself together properly and organize his life in such a way as to exploit his talents to the maximum.

The woman is far more realistic and "earthy" than he is, so she can help him realize his ambitions.

The final combination of the numbers is 2, which means that the relationship will work toward achieving the aims of the woman, who does things for the good of her partner.

It is a complementary relationship that is excellent for both parties. In addition, their sexuality is very good.

The rating on the numerological scale of love: 10-

A number 4 woman with a number 8 man

A number 8 man is also searching for loyal and trustworthy security. The woman "doubles" her properties in the figure of the man, and entrusts herself to him with eyes closed.

This means that in this kind of relationship, the man is the leader. In this shared unit (whose combination is 12), there is a strong emphasis on the family unit, cooperative creativity, and continuity.

This relationship will not break up because the combination of powers in it is tremendous. The relationship between the members of the couple is excellent, even if there is a lack of spontaneity, and it tends to be a more calculated and orderly one.

The rating on the numerological scale of love: 9

A number 4 woman with a number 9 man

A number 9 man is the diametric opposite of the number 4 woman. The combination of their numbers is 4 (that is, $4 + 9 = 13$, $1 + 3 = 4$). This attests to the fact that the woman will want the relationship to be run along her lines and according to her will, and she will seek to be the one in control.

In order for things to run in this way, the man must make concessions to an extent that he is liable to interpret as defeatism. Only if the number 4 woman finds a number 9 man whose masculine properties are not so dominant, and who will be willing to let her be the leader, will she have found the prince of her dreams.

In general, this doesn't happen, and although their sexual relationship is superb, the man who is bound in the number 4 woman's ropes tends to rebel and break out.

The rating on the numerological scale of love: 7

The number 5 woman

A number 5 woman with a number 1 man

The number 5 woman is focused on herself and on her femininity. In every relationship, she will search for whatever makes it easier for her to get what she wants, and to fulfill herself and her aspirations. The number 1 man finds in the number 5 woman everything he ever wanted in a woman, except fidelity. The combination of 1 and 5 is 6, which follows its components. Since the woman has the advantage in the combination, it is easier for her to steer 6 to her purposes.

This combination is not suitable for any kind of partnership other than a romantic one. In the personal realm, it is the winning one. She has the ability to demonstrate her abundant femininity, while he is masculine enough not to feel threatened by this in any way, or to lose his feeling of superiority. Despite the fact that the occasional problem can arise, it will certainly be a viable, potentially long-lasting relationship.

The rating on the numerological scale of love: 7

A number 5 woman with a number 2 man

The strong and dominant number 5 woman conquers the number 2 man with his slightly feminine characteristics, and causes him to be a loyal and obedient mate at her side.

She is the leader of the relationship, so its nature depends on her will. It can be excellent and fruitful if the woman learns to cooperate with her partner in all areas, and allows him space to express himself and exploit his talents and abilities. If she dominates him completely, and lets herself go overboard, she will spoil the quality of their relationship.

This is a relationship that is more successful on the business or economic level than on the personal level.

The rating on the numerological scale of love: 7

A number 5 woman with a number 3 man

The number 3 man will fulfill the number 5 woman's wishes and realize her long-term ambitions; for this reason, it is a good relationship. Their combination produces 8, which indicates infinity, persistence. The number 3 man loves to initiate and create, and seeks an opportunity for cooperative development. He has a flexible personality, and is prepared to adapt himself to the number 5 woman and make concessions in their relationship.

She finds this relationship excellent, mainly because of the fact that she needs a degree of stability that the number 3 man can give her, and she knows that a relationship like this will allow her to develop, and will not tie her down. It is a good relationship from the personal and sexual point of view, and is excellent for any business or other partnership, including establishing a family.

The rating on the numerological scale of love: 8+

A number 5 woman with a number 5 man

This is a fatal combination with an unequivocal answer: NO!

On the one hand, the number 5 woman is strong and self-focused, and enjoys being occupied with fulfilling her ambitions. On the other, the number 5 man is selfish and places himself at the center of the universe. The clash resulting from this kind of relationship is completely predictable.

The two members of the couple don't stop fighting with each other about everything.

There is not a moment that one of them doesn't feel that the other is demanding all the attention, and neither of them is willing to give in. The only realm in which they get along is the sexual realm, and even here both of them would be delighted to cheat on the other, just to make the other one into a cuckold.

The rating on the numerological scale of love: 4
...and that's the lowest number on the numerological scale!

A number 5 woman with a number 6 man

This is a combination of convenience. The man is a stable type with a tendency toward obstinacy. He knows how to stand up for himself at almost any price. Having said that, he is also blessed with initiative and vision.

The number 5 woman is strong, and values these qualities in her partner. She is aware that they can help her, and that they can constitute a convenient basis for her development.

The number 6 man knows how to make do with what she can give him, without demanding more, and he is definitely grateful for what he has.

The rating on the numerological scale of love: 6

A number 5 woman with a number 7 man

The number 7 man is not exactly a guy whose feet are planted firmly in reality. He is a bit spaced out, and the strong and ambitious number 5 woman knows that she won't get far with him as far as accomplishing the objectives she has set herself is concerned.

They operate on completely different wavelengths. While she is down-to-earth and practical, he is interested things spiritual.

The lack of communication between them is expressed on all levels – personal, business, and economic. They live on two parallel lines that will never meet, either emotionally or mentally.

The rating on the numerological scale of love: 4+

A number 5 woman with a number 8 man

The number 8 man is a square, stable type. Surprisingly, the relationship between him and the number 5 woman is excellent. The number 8 man has the ability to move things from the theoretical plane to the practical plane. He can make dreams into reality, and establish the foundations of the new reality on firm ground, for a long time. And this is exactly what the number 5 woman wants and needs.

The properties of the number 5 woman, which others perceive as negative – her selfishness, her being shockingly extreme and down-to-earth – are interpreted as being greatly advantageous by the number 8 man. He uses her intuition to hone his business sense, enjoys her abundant femininity, and rejoices in her.

Having said that, he does not see her as a sexual object, but rather relates to the sum total of her qualities as a person.

The number 5 woman is grateful to him for that, and consequently this relationship will be long-lasting.

The rating on the numerological scale of love: 9-

A number 5 woman with a number 9 man

The number 9 man expects his partner to be his personal guide in the labyrinth of life. She, the somewhat selfish woman who focuses on herself, finds it difficult to get into someone else's skin – as her number 9 partner expects her to.

The number 9 man finds the number 5 woman much more perfect than others see her, and he hopes that she will project a large amount of her traits into the family unit.

They have a good interpersonal relationship, but a relationship in which there are utilitarian considerations, such as a business or entrepreneurial partnership, will not succeed, since the tension between them will increase and their relations will deteriorate.

The rating on the numerological scale of love: 7

The number 6 woman

A number 6 woman with a number 1 man

The number 6 woman knows how to find equilibrium in life. She can be both romantic and assertive to the correct extent; she knows how to develop herself and to fulfill her ambitions and goals, but at the same time does not stand in her partner's way, and gives him the space he needs. The number 6 woman finds everything she is lacking in the number 1 man: initiative, creativity, and the characteristic properties of masculinity.

The partnership between them will most likely be balanced; it won't be the kind that deviates from accepted frameworks. They always fulfill the expectations of the people around them, and always reflect public opinion. The danger in such a relationship is a certain dependency of the woman on the man, and this is liable to lead to a break-up. If she takes the trouble to find things to occupy herself with outside of the framework of the family unity, she can be more confident of her independence.

The rating on the numerological scale of love: 8-

A number 6 woman with a number 2 man

The combination of the two produces 8, which, as we have said before, is a strong and unbreakable one. In this combination, the weight of the woman is the decisive one. The number 2 man is blessed with properties of giving, nurturing, and readiness to help – properties that are perceived as "feminine."

Since the number 6 woman is multifaceted, and knows how to balance her life in various realms, she knows how to include the man in her life in such a way that with his help, she will achieve stability and constancy in life – properties that she lacks.

It must be mentioned that the number 6 woman's willingness to build the family unit with the number 2 man derive from a rational standpoint that reflects utilitarian considerations. While their sexuality lacks tension, and will be a bit boring, the number 6 woman will accept the situation willingly, as long as she knows that the rest of the areas of her life are being run as she wants, according to her plan.

The rating on the numerological scale of love: 8+

A number 6 woman with a number 3 man

This is a combination that makes life difficult for both parties. The number 3 man dominates it. In a number 3 man, the combination of man and woman dominates. He is a man who is not prepared to accept the domination of the number 6 woman, who likes to control the relationship. He will do everything to determine his own way of life, and not let her interfere in it.

Having said that, he will soon discover that he eventually reaches the very point to which the woman aspired. And in any case, both of them ultimately do what the woman set her sights on from the outset.

When they cooperate, there can be wonderful harmony between them, and the cooperation will lead to the fruits of great success. However, the numerous tensions that exist between them are also liable to destroy the relationship (and that is what almost always happens in the end) in a tremendous blow-up.

The rating on the numerological scale of love: 7-

A number 6 woman with a number 4 man

The combination of the number 6 woman with a number 4 man produces the number 1. This is a difficult relationship. The number 6 woman finds herself in a relationship with a square number 4 man who can only give her stability and order in life. She doesn't need this, because she herself is well balanced, and this gives her life a great deal of stability. Sometimes she stops and asks herself: What does this man in my life actually give me – or what can he give me? She doesn't always like the inevitable answer, so this relationship stumbles along, almost from the beginning, to failure.

The rating on the numerological scale of love: 5

A number 6 woman with a number 5 man

The number 5 man is selfish, as we have said before. He admires himself and his traits, sometimes to the point of self-adoration, and knows exactly what he is looking for in a partner.

The combination of the two is 11, that is, 2, which gives the woman an edge, and turns her into the more decisive and dominant element in this relationship.

Predictably, this is not to the number 5 man's liking, and he is ready to dump her forthwith – anything rather than have her walk all over him. In fact, it is generally the number 5 man who breaks off the relationship abruptly, before the number 6 woman realizes what's happening.

Ultimately, this is the correct thing for both parties, because next time round, each one will find a partner who is more suitable for him/her.

The rating on the numerological scale of love: 5

A number 6 woman with a number 6 man

This is a perfect combination, especially for the woman, who sees before her a man whose ambitions are the same as hers. Each member of the couple plays an equal role in the relationship, so that neither one feels exploited or frustrated. On the contrary – each one contributes his/her abilities to the relationship. They build each other up and complement their qualities without detracting from each other's ambitions.

The relationship will succeed whether it is only a business-economic relationship or a personal one. They operate in coordination, and this unstoppable coordination can be compared to a wagon whose wheels all move in sync.

The rating on the numerological scale of love: 9+

A number 6 woman with a number 7 man

This combination is doomed to total failure. Contrary to the combination of the number 6 woman and the number 6 man, who operate in almost perfect coordination, the combination of the number 6 woman with the number 7 man cannot suit the needs, wishes, ambitions, or expectations of the number 6 woman, who is so totally different than him on all planes. A waste of time...

The rating on the numerological scale of love: 4

A number 6 woman with a number 8 man

This is a successful and enduring combination. The number 6 woman finds herself in a relationship that helps her nurture her ambitions and fulfill her wishes.

Because of the combination of the numbers 6 + 8 = 14, and 1 + 4 = 5, this attests to an almost unbreakable relationship.

If there is a break-up, it will not be caused by one of the parties, but rather by objective reasons.

Having said that, it is a relationship that is more successful in mutual business endeavors than in interpersonal relationships, where there is still room for improvement.

The rating on the numerological scale of love: 8-

A number 6 woman with a number 9 man

This is a perfect relationship, and it is difficult (or rather, almost impossible) to find one like it. The number 6 woman is not attracted to the number 9 man only because of the harmony that prevails among their common properties, and the perfection with which they can function together – but also because she is powerfully attracted to him sexually. She is bewitched by him!

This is the man who complements the number 6 woman's properties at a slightly higher level than hers. It is a relationship in which there is a kind of perfect balance between the members of the couple, and they reach the perfect realization of their ambitions – both material and personal.

The rating on the numerological scale of love: 10

The number 7 woman

A number 7 woman with a number 1 man

The number 7 woman has an open mind. She is liberal, and open to change and innovation.

She is curious, inquiring, and intelligent, and is one of those types that is always looking for themselves.

The number 7 is a strong essential number that can develop in any direction of human endeavor.

Women whose number is 7 always feel the need to prove themselves and succeed in whatever they do.

This property is common to the number 7 woman and the number 1 man, who also has a fierce urge to succeed and to display his success publicly. They are both ambitious people who can push each other forward, and make each other fruitful.

If they are able to do all this in the right dosage, without disturbing their partner, and without making him/her feel threatened, the relationship will be successful. It is possible that their first years together will not be a bed of roses, but after they learn to find the good in every situation, and to separate the wheat from the chaff, their path to success will be assured.

The rating on the numerological scale of love: 8+

A number 7 woman with a number 2 man

The number 2 man represents, as we have mentioned, feminine properties. Number 7 women don't lack these properties. On the contrary – she needs a man with typical masculine properties to be her helpmeet.

The sexual relationship between the two is not brilliant. Despite the fact that the number 2 man is sensitive and considerate, the number 7 woman will interpret this to mean that he is constantly searching for her weak points, and she won't stand this for long.

This is a woman whose life is full, and she does not need a partner to fill the void or to complement her properties. She is very sensitive, but at the same time career-oriented and feminine.

She is at one with herself and sees no contradiction in the situation. This means that a man who is unable to fulfill her true needs does not count for anything in her eyes, and it would be a pity to waste her time with him.

The rating on the numerological scale of love: 6-

A number 7 woman with a number 3 man

This is the man that the number 7 woman is looking for. His personality contains both masculine and feminine properties. They are on the same wavelength and immediately sense their compatibility. They look at the world from the same point of view, they are both curious and inquiring about it, and there is instant chemistry between them.

The combination of their numbers yields the number 10, a number that moves us from a lower rung to a higher rung on the numerological ladder. In other words, the combination of these two people will cause them to reach a higher plane in their lives.

Together they will be able to establish new frontiers and realize their ambitions, and more. This is a very good relationship, from the sexual point of view as well, and will remain stable for many years.

The rating on the numerological scale of love: 9 (even 9+)

A number 7 woman with a number 4 man

This is an unthinkable relationship since the properties of both parties clash. The number 4 man has all the properties that the number 7 woman avoids like the plague: he is square, orderly, and "establishment," while she is original and open-minded, and loves change and surprises.

The number 4 man wants a quiet, obedient woman who knows her place in the home, basic security being more important to him than anything else. The number 7 woman is built differently. She cannot be the little submissive woman standing at the stove and waiting for her husband to come home from work.

Only very infrequently can a relationship like this succeed, and then only on condition that the number 4 man can let the number 7 woman expand her world and her horizons.

However, it hardly ever happens, mainly because there are very few number 7 women who would agree to sacrifice themselves for a partner like this.

The rating on the numerological scale of love: 6

A number 7 woman with a number 5 man

The combination $5 + 7 = 12$, $1 + 2 = 3$ tends toward the woman, so that despite the number 5 man's selfishness, there could be equilibrium between the two.

The second possibility is that the number 5 man, who is preoccupied with himself and with fulfilling his goals and ambitions, will not agree to give the number 7 woman the attention she needs, and then all hell breaks loose!

The rating on the numerological scale of love: 7

A number 7 woman with a number 6 man

The number 6 man is a man who can adapt. He has the ability to take two opposites and turn them into a whole.

He can be the perfect partner for a number 7 woman because he will support her emotionally and materially, and will go through flood and fire for her for a long time. Despite the fact that he gives so much to her, he does not feel deprived, and this is the secret of this long-standing relationship.

The number 6 man is also enthusiastic in bed, and the number 7 woman's life is not boring for a second. He is a genuine partner in every aspect of her life, to the point that without him, she has a hard time functioning.

The rating on the numerological scale of love: 9

A number 7 woman with a number 7 man

The combination of the two is 14, that is, $1 + 4 = 5$. This hints that the two are not destined to work together, especially in the business-economic sphere. The relationship is doomed to failure, and can even be destructive.

In contrast, on the level of matters of the heart, it is a very good combination. The number 7 man is a man after the number 7 woman's heart, and from an emotional point of view, they feel on top of the world together!

However, their relations are generally not perfect because of the simple fact that most of the time, they do not differentiate between the world of love and emotion and the real material world. This "conflict" between the two worlds is liable to cause a real crisis in their relations. If they learn to ignore their desire for a relationship that goes beyond the sexual-personal, they can have an excellent relationship.

The rating on the numerological scale of love: 8

A number 7 woman with a number 8 man

The relationship between a number 7 woman with a number 8 man is quite good in all aspects and spheres of life. They are sufficiently flexible to adapt to each other's paths, so their relationship is successful.

The number 8 man can wait for however long it takes to reach the stability and serenity that he seeks. The number 7 woman is the one who will lead their relationship, but the adaptable number 8 man will not see this as a threat to his role in it.

Their sexuality is not perfect, but the end results of their relationship are very good, and speak for themselves.

The rating on the numerological scale of love: 8

A number 7 woman with a number 9 man

The common path of the number 7 woman and the number 9 man can be extremely successful in everything to do with business, economic, or creative cooperation.

In contrast, there will be problems in the interpersonal sphere: the number 9 man will feel exploited in this relationship, and will not derive happiness from it. He will almost certainly break off the relationship at a certain stage, and walk away. Only if there is excellent cooperation between the two in the other spheres of life will it be possible to bridge the gap in the personal aspect.

Another thing that binds them is the fact that they present a totally united front against danger or an outside threat. They join forces and go out to defend themselves against the "enemy."

The rating on the numerological scale of love: 8+

The number 8 woman

A number 8 woman with a number 1 man

The number 8 woman is different than other women from the point of view of the numerological compatibility of the numbers of love.

Unlike the others, she is not "influenced" by the personal number of her partner, and it is almost insignificant as far as she is concerned. She is different because of her very great self-confidence.

The number 8 woman and the number 1 man both find themselves galloping toward their goals in an attempt to accomplish as many as possible, and their achievements are significant.

If the two decide to be business partners, it is a winning combination. The same goes for sex. However, in anything to do with personal relations they will find it difficult to function together, cooperatively and mutually, especially if there are extreme differences in mentality.

The rating on the numerological scale of love: 8

A number 8 woman with a number 2 man

The number 8 woman contains the numbers 2 and 4. Taking this into account, as well as the fact that the number 2 man is considered to have feminine properties, there is a clear-cut conclusion: She is a strong woman facing a submissive man. She is very dominant in their relations while he tags along after her obediently, or, alternatively, is her sworn admirer.

Such a relationship can only be successful if the woman looks for a man with whom she can feel comfortable at home, without constantly being on her guard.

The number 8 woman can be satisfied with the number 2 man only in things concerning raising the children or looking after the home. All the rest – the cooperation between them, their sexuality, and even the ability to learn from each other how each one can develop – is rather weak.

The rating on the numerological scale of love: 7-

A number 8 woman with a number 3 man

At a certain point in the relationship between the number 8 woman and the manipulative number 3 man, the woman is liable to feel that she has been deceived by her partner.

In the beginning, she felt that she was in control of the relationship – the dominant factor in it (helped by the combination 11, which is the feminine 2). However, after a time, she wises up and sees that with slow, sure, and determined steps, the number 3 man has conquered her, and she finds herself being led by her partner rather than being the leader. Love plays an important role here, so she does not object to the new situation she finds herself in. The couple can expect a happy life, filled with blooming romance, a family, and children. If the woman feels threatened at a certain point, feeling that she has lost her clout in the relationship, she may want out.

The rating on the numerological scale of love: 7-

A number 8 woman with a number 4 man

The number 4 man has "half" of the number 8 woman's number, and this is the basis of the relationship between them. The man will never outdo any of the woman's properties in any field. Even so, there are many such relationships that are successful. The basis for success generally lies in the fact that the number 8 woman is the embodiment of all the number 4 man's ambitions. Although she is better than he is in almost all fields, he is at one with the relationship, and admires her with all his heart and soul.

She will always be the one who maps the path, while he serves as her "anchor." Their personal relations will be comfortable and relaxed, although lacking in excitement and sometimes boring for the number 8 woman.

The rating on the numerological scale of love: 7

A number 8 woman with a number 5 man

There is no special compatibility between the selfish, egocentric, self-adoring number 5 man and the number 8 woman who is well aware of her abilities and strength. She is not especially attracted to any of the number 5 man's properties. If such a relationship were likely, it would mainly be based on sexuality, because the number 8 woman may be conquered by the number 5 man's charms just because of his exploits in bed. Very soon, when she discovers his selfishness, and their sex life has burnt itself out, she will dump him.

The rating on the numerological scale of love: 5+ (temporarily!)

A number 8 woman with a number 6 man

There is almost perfect compatibility here. The number 6 man knows what he wants and how to get it. The number 8 woman's properties are similar to his. What makes their relationship long-lived is the distribution of roles between them: each one is aware of his own and the other one's strengths, and they divide up the fields of action between them. Like this, they create opportunities to operate jointly in both the business and personal realms. A relationship like this goes on for years, and improves with the passage of time.

The rating on the numerological scale of love: 9

A number 8 woman with a number 7 man

Although we're talking about a relationship between the active, practical, and ambitious number 8 woman and the "spaced out" number 7 man, in most cases we find that it is patently successful. The reason is that they complement each other's properties.

The practical woman sees to all the concrete daily needs of the home, while her partner, who also shares the burden, adds a dash of "color" to their lives, introducing the conceptual, cerebral, and visionary aspects. They both know their function, and do not try to "invade" the other person's territory.

The only case in which the relationship may founder is if, over the years, one of the couple develops in such a way that an unbridgeable gap is created. This could happen with many other couples as well, of course.

The rating on the numerological scale of love: 8

A number 8 woman with a number 8 man

This is the worst possible combination. There is no chance of cooperation or of mutual relations. On the contrary: the two come from standpoints that are constantly at loggerheads.

Their situation can be compared to two cars on a narrow bridge, where neither one is willing to reverse and let the other one cross the bridge. This relationship is full of tensions. It is a constant struggle, which causes a lack of confidence in both sides, and undermines each one's status and ability to succeed in life.

There is almost no field in which there could be any reasonable cooperation between the two – not on the business, creative, personal, or sexual level.

The rating on the numerological scale of love: 4

A number 8 woman with a number 9 man

This is a relationship in which the number 8 woman exerts an overwhelming influence on the development of the relationship, mainly because of the combination $8 + 9 = 17$, $1 + 7 = 8$.

Despite the number 8 woman's dominance, the number 9 man does not feel threatened. On the contrary, he gives her full credit, helps her along her path, supports her, and is a helpmeet to her all the way, even if her path is a very long one. There is no trace of envy or jealousy of the other person's development in this kind of relationship.

The relationship is good and fruitful. It is excellent on all levels – business-economic, personal, and sexual.

The rating on the numerological scale of love: 9+

The number 9 woman

A number 9 woman with a number 1 man

The number 9 cancels itself out in every possible numerological combination. For this reason, the number 9 woman will always be totally influenced by the man with her, and will efface herself for him.

Having said that, she is blessed with talents, and because of her special properties, she can adapt to every situation, find the good in everything, and avoid unnecessary strife.

The combination of the number 9 woman with the number 1 man creates 1 again (9 + 1 = 10; 1 + 0 = 1). In other words, the dominant one in the relationship is the man.

The properties of the number 1 man are very masculine. As such, he will want a loyal woman who will always stand at his side, and whose goals and desires will fit in with his. The number 9 woman will have no trouble doing this.

In anything to do with business ties, he will be the entrepreneur and she will be the actual manager who helps and supports. While their interpersonal and sexual relations may lack equality, this will not necessarily bother the number 9 woman. In any case, if there is ever a crisis in their relationship, it will stem from the sexual or personal realm.

The rating on the numerological scale of love: 8

A number 9 woman with a number 2 man

As we have mentioned before, the dominant properties of the number 2 man are feminine. He will want to please the number 9 woman, and will look to her for direction, and she will want to please him.

This is a warm relationship in which both members of the couple are very considerate and attentive of each other's needs – sometimes perhaps overly so, because there is no one to "lead" the relationship. Sometimes we find a couple like this who are happy together, but lack initiative, and are stuck in a rut.

It is very characteristic of such a couple to consider their offspring as the embodiment of their self-realization, and direct all their resources toward satisfying the demands and wishes of their children.

The rating on the numerological scale of love: 9-

A number 9 woman with a number 3 man

The number 3 man has many of the number 9 woman's properties, since 9 is a multiple of 3.

Although we would expect an ideal relationship because of this, both parties are actually limited by this combination.

The rules of the game are strict, and the man tends to blame his partner repeatedly. She, for her part, tries to placate him in her way, so she operates in a different manner every time – until he considers her to be an unstable, capricious woman.

The relationship will be problematic, both on the business level (a real disaster) and on the interpersonal level, where endless arguments and misunderstandings will occur. Only on the sexual level can there be any harmony between them.

The rating on the numerological scale of love: 6-

A number 9 woman with a number 4 man

The number 4 man is searching for stability and security in life, and especially a warm, stable family unit. The number 9 woman has no difficulty fitting into this kind of relationship, and does it very well and with the best intentions.

Even if the man is the more dominant one at the beginning of the relationship, over the course of time, after the relationship has become established and after the number 9 woman has proved the sincerity of her intentions and her desire for a long-term relationship, the man will trust her more, and she will eventually take his place.

If there is a serious crisis between them, it will be on the sexual level, since the number 4 man has limited sexual horizons, and the number 9 woman, when she is mature and experienced, is aware of his limitations, and feels frustrated.

The rating on the numerological scale of love: 7

A number 9 woman with a number 5 man

The number 5 man is selfish and self-centered. He needs someone who can put him in his place, "ground" him, and get him back into reality. Instead of that, he finds an adoring admirer beside him, who responds "yes" to his every whim.

Very quickly, the number 9 woman will find herself enslaved to the number 5 man. This is liable to make him relate to her pejoratively and disrespectfully. The relationship is one-sided, and causes the number 9 woman to lose any measure of independence and desire for self-realization or for nurturing her own ambitions. It is painful and unnecessary.

The rating on the numerological scale of love: 4+

A number 9 woman with a number 6 man

The number 6 man relates to his partner first and foremost as a goal, a target. He contains a mixture of giving and an ability to receive in return.

He is settled and considerate, and in his relationship with a number 9 woman, he will not be afraid of giving up his path and adopting hers. He tries his best to please her, and she, for her part, can only rejoice in such a relationship, where her pride and self-respect as a woman and as a person are preserved intact.

Their interpersonal and sexual relationship is excellent, and generally continues for many years. This is one of the only relationships that the number 9 woman can establish with a man in which she does not feel subjugated to him, but rather equal.

The only problem here is their lack of initiative in spheres that are not interpersonal, and this is liable to lead to a state of boredom and stagnation.

The rating on the numerological scale of love: 8-

A number 9 woman with a number 7 man

The number 7 man is a bit "spaced out." This is the reason that in this particular relationship, the number 9 woman will be the strong, powerful partner. The number 7 man wants someone who he can lean on, and who will help him fulfill his vocation. The number 9 woman does this well. By taking the responsibility and most of the burden upon herself, she will find a way to give her partner the opportunity to make the most of himself. Because the number 7 man wants his partner to make the most of herself as well, the number 9 woman takes care of her own wishes, too. In this way, the desires of both parties, as well as their personalities and needs, are expressed. The number 9 woman realizes herself at the side of her partner, who in turn feels that his partner is giving him a great deal of support. Their sexuality is also good – sometimes even excellent.

The rating on the numerological scale of love: 9+

A number 9 woman with a number 8 man

The number 8 man, the "squared square" (twice 4), tends to ignore the number 9 woman and her efforts to build a good and stable relationship. While she can endure being humiliated or deprecated sometimes, there is no way that she can stand being ignored. She is not masochistic by nature. It is difficult for the number 8 man to understand the number 9 woman's motives and behavior, and if any channel of communication opens between them, it will be completely futile.

They do not get along in the creative realm or in the personal realm. Their sexuality is also weak.

The rating on the numerological scale of love: 5

A number 9 woman with a number 9 man

Everything the number 9 man does, he does for himself. Since the number 9 woman will do everything for the man who is with her, both of them work toward satisfying the desires of the number 9 man. From the point of view of the number 9 woman, this is a one-sided relationship in which she gives everything without getting anything in return. This relationship is very reminiscent of the one with a number 5 man. On the other hand, in the sexual realm, the two are champions. But that isn't enough. There is no doubt that the constant feeling of deprivation in which the number 9 woman lives will not allow the relationship to continue for any length of time.

The rating on the numerological scale of love: 6